PERFORMANCE, DANCE AND POLITICAL ECONOMY

Interdisciplinary Book Series
Dance in Dialogue
Series Editors: Anita Gonzalez, Katerina Paramana, and Victoria Thoms

The Interdisciplinary Book Series *Dance in Dialogue* critically examines the relations between Performance, Dance, and other disciplines. It fosters interdisciplinary approaches, cross-disciplinary exchanges, and conversation as a mode of knowledge production. The series aims to offer new ways of interrogating the relation of performance and dance to other disciplines and to the political, cultural, social, and economic issues and contexts in and in relation to they are created, presented, and theorised.

We seek to challenge the ways in which scholarship has been traditionally represented and disseminated, critically explore the dialogical relationship between theory and practice, and foster the ethos of collaboration, dialogue, and political engagement that is needed for vibrant knowledge production within and outside of academia. We encourage experimentation in publication format and research developed through innovative forms of collaborative and collective working across different modes of disciplinary and interdisciplinary inquiry and dissemination.

To realise this vision, the series offers two distinct publication formats via two strands:

In Conversation
   A collection of short books that present radical thinking emerging from curated conversations between the body(ies) / performance / dance / choreography and another discipline, area of research, field of knowledge or practice on topical artistic, cultural, and political issues. Written by leading thinkers (artists and scholars) who critically explore the insights the different areas of knowledge and practice offer into one another, as well as the affordances, potentials, and implications of these insights for the contemporary world, these approximately 40,000-word

books typically develop out of international conversation events and are published within approximately a year after them.

Moving Forward

A collection of cutting-edge and forward-thinking, full-length monographs and edited collections that challenge understandings of the body(ies)/performance/dance/choreography and its (their) relation to political, cultural, and socioeconomic issues and contexts, foster dialogue and interdisciplinarity, and critically explore the relationship between theory and practice.

Other titles in the series

In Conversation titles:

Dance, Architecture and Engineering
Adesola Akinleye

Moving Forward titles:
The Choreopolitics of Alain Platel's Les Ballets C de la B: Emotions, Gestures, Politics
Edited by Christel Stalpaert, Guy Cools and Hildegard De Vuyst

FALLING through dance and life
Emilyn Claid

PERFORMANCE, DANCE AND POLITICAL ECONOMY

Bodies at the End of the World

**Edited by
Katerina Paramana
and Anita Gonzalez**

BLOOMSBURY ACADEMIC
LONDON • NEW YORK • OXFORD • NEW DELHI • SYDNEY

BLOOMSBURY ACADEMIC
Bloomsbury Publishing Plc
50 Bedford Square, London, WC1B 3DP, UK
1385 Broadway, New York, NY 10018, USA
29 Earlsfort Terrace, Dublin 2, Ireland

BLOOMSBURY, BLOOMSBURY ACADEMIC and the Diana logo are trademarks
of Bloomsbury Publishing Plc

First published in Great Britain 2021
Paperback edition published 2022

Copyright © Katerina Paramana, Anita Gonzalez, and contributors 2021, 2022

Katerina Paramana, Anita Gonzalez, and contributors have asserted
their right under the Copyright, Designs and Patents Act, 1988,
to be identified as Authors of this work.

For legal purposes the Acknowledgments on p. xi constitute an extension
of this copyright page.

Dance in Dialogue is an initiative developed with the support of the Society for
Dance Research (Registered Charity No. 286595).

Cover design: Charlotte Daniels
Cover image: nibia pastrana santiago, *danza actual o el evento
coreográfico: estructuras temporales para provocar un evento
imposible*, 2015. Photo by Tony Cruz

All rights reserved. No part of this publication may be reproduced
or transmitted in any form or by any means, electronic or mechanical,
including photocopying, recording, or any information storage or
retrieval system, without prior permission in writing from the publishers.

Bloomsbury Publishing Plc does not have any control over, or
responsibility for, any third-party websites referred to or in this book.
All internet addresses given in this book were correct at the time of
going to press. The author and publisher regret any inconvenience
caused if addresses have changed or sites have ceased to exist, but
can accept no responsibility for any such changes.

A catalogue record for this book is available from the British Library.

A catalog record for this book is available from the Library of Congress.

ISBN: HB: 978-1-3501-8869-3
PB: 978-1-3501-8875-4
ePDF: 978-1-3501-8871-6
eBook: 978-1-3501-8870-9

Series: Dance in Dialogue

Typeset by Deanta Global Publishing Services, Chennai, India

To find out more about our authors and books visit www.bloomsbury.com and
sign up for our newsletters.

CONTENTS

List of Figures x
Acknowledgments xi

Foreword: A Gesture xii
Tavia Nyong'o

Opening Thoughts and Introductions 1
Katerina Paramana and Anita Gonzalez

Provocations 15

1 Performance, Dance and Political Economy: A Provocation 17
Katerina Paramana

2 Recognizing Race and Class in Dance: Gonzalez Response to Paramana 32
Anita Gonzalez

Dialogue 1: *Control of Bodies* 39

3 A World beyond the Captured Body 41
Nina Power

4 Choreographing Rage 46
Marc Arthur

Dialogue 2: *Commodification of Bodies* 53

5 Honesty and the Body 55
Nina Power

6 Feeling My Way Through Several Beginnings 62
Alexandrina Hemsley

Dialogue 3: *Rest, Productivity and Survival* 69

7 Sleepwalking: Toward a New Corporeality of Dance 71
Marc Arthur

8 It Only Happens in Daylight 79
Jamila Johnson-Small

Dialogue 4: *Communal Disruptions* 89

9 Community, Coloniality and *Convivencia* in the Festival de Danza de Santa María la Antigua del Darién, Colombia 91
Melissa Blanco Borelli

10 Changing Our Bodies' Relationships to Reality 101
Usva Seregina

Dialogue 5: *Anarchic Inversions of Neoliberal Economies* 109

11 The "End," "Lived Time" or How to Say Goodbye to Your World, A World 111
Melissa Blanco Borelli

12 Dance, Anarchism, Mutual Aid 119
Elena Loizidou

Dialogue 6: *Escaping Capitalism?* 131

13 Breaking the Illusion of Reality: Exploring Reiterations of the Performance of Consumption 133
Usva Seregina

14 From Exchange to Freedom and Back: No Guarantees 143
Elena Loizidou

Group Conversation 149

15 In Conversation—Performance, Dance and Political Economy: Bodies at the End of the World 151
Katerina Paramana, Anita Gonzalez, Nina Power, Marc Arthur, Melissa Blanco Borelli, Usva Seregina, Jamila Johnson-Small, Elena Loizidou, and Alexandrina Hemsley

Notes on Contributors 181
About the Editors 183
Index 185

FIGURES

1 (Ch. 4) ACT UP "Seize Control of the FDA" action at the Food and Drug Administration headquarters in Rockville, Maryland, on October 11, 1988. Photo by T. L. Litt 47

2 (Ch. 10) *Spatial Confessions* by Bojana Cvejić and Christine De Smedt, Turbine Hall, Tate Modern, 2014. Photo by Lennart Laberenz 102

3–4 (Ch. 11) nibia pastrana santiago, Tara (Golden Retriever) and seagrape, *danza actual o el evento coreográfico: estructuras temporales para provocar un evento imposible (Current dance or the choreographic event: temporary structures to provoke an impossible event)*, 2015, Casa del Sargento Beta-Local, San Juan, Puerto Rico. Photo: Tony Cruz 115

5 (Ch. 14) *Exchange* choreographed by Merce Cunningham (1978). Merce Cunningham Dance © Lois Greenfield 146

ACKNOWLEDGMENTS

We would like to thank our contributors for embracing this dialogical exchange and for their time and insights. Our thanks also to the Society for Dance Research for their support of this project and to our series co-editor, Victoria Thoms, for her support and insightful comments on the manuscript.

KATERINA PARAMANA AND ANITA GONZALEZ

FOREWORD
A GESTURE
Tavia Nyong'o

The chapters and dialogues on performance and dance in the expanded field collected in this book seek to imagine and enact a movement beyond the constraints of capitalism. This is a utopian gesture of refusal, refusing what is in order to picture what might yet be.[1] And not just to picture what might be but to feel it, not just as a solitary vision but in concert, a collective fantasia that is a mutual undoing of the carapace that we each built up against attuning to the possibility that something could change, that the other shoe could drop, that the final straw could break the back of our collective tolerance for the intolerable. Here, in the swirl and stillness of pandemic time, here, amid the uprising of the dispossessed in a street choreography of protest against state violence, we are invited to reflect, yet again, on the crucial stakes of putting our bodies on the line.

Reflecting on the aspirations of this book to reenchant a world of corporeal possibility currently occupied by the strangulating science of political economy, I am reminded of that great dancer-theorist, Sylvia Wynter, who reminded us that (racial) capitalism is a cultural as well as economic system, and that one cannot hope to revolutionize the one without, in and through the same gesture, revolutionizing the other. By provincializing *homo oeconomicus*, Wynter invites us to correct for the overrepresentation of Man, and to remember all the ways of being, all the ways of moving, that the coloniality of being failed to extirpate.[2] She asks us to begin again, and tell the story of aesthetics differently, decentering Western bias and reenchanting the process of becoming human on a truly planetary scale. She tells us that the legacy of the oppressed has been to never relinquish this resource: the body. This is to say, Wynter invites us to acknowledge, with Jacqueline Shea Murphy, that the people have never stopped dancing.[3] But what does it mean to say this? What does it mean to step, leap, or fly toward a decolonial horizon as the stewards of a warming planet?

Capitalist realism insists that we cannot see beyond corners, that the response to disaster is always and only to find new ways to further develop and exploit our bodies as human capital under whichever latest cruel twist in the incarnations of neoliberalism.[4] Dance as a discipline, somewhat infamously, is sometimes held culpable in this willingness to resculpt the body to fit the capitalist mold. André Lepecki warns us of the choreopolice, or a generalization of the capacity to monitor and punish any who step out of line.[5] But he invites us to counter the choreopolice with a choreopolitics, and this invitation only resonates and expands across this book's commitment to always think the political and the economic in tandem. Given the way in which the spaces of the economic (especially matters of consumption) are so often privatized, domesticated, and deemed pre- or apolitical, I sense something strongly feminist in this insistence on political economy. We may not need a term as ungainly as choreo-politico-economics to do this feminist work for us, but we do certainly need the range of feminist, queer, Black, brown, and minoritarian work that this book brings together.

The utopian impulse in the buzz and rumble of Black diasporic social dance forms, Jayna Brown argues, no longer requires routing through Eurocentric frames of analysis, if ever they did.[6] The wretched of the earth are doing their own damned thing. We can only hope to fall into step, analytically speaking, with these joyous and angular socialities. As knowledge is eclipsed by information, and discipline is overwhelmed by data, it's increasingly unclear what exactly the old ethnographic approaches would be doing anyway. To say this is to concede nothing to the rise of intelligent machines, still less to buy into a scenario in which automation frees up time for rest, recreation, and creativity. The enforced idleness of some during the quarantine (enabled by the obligatory endangerment of other "essential workers") revealed that free time, alone, is not what is stopping the revolution. A year without dance, theater, music, and even museums is an excellent opportunity to pause and reflect on what might come out on the other side. But the confidence that there will be an other side must increasingly be seen as a matter of privilege. For many, for most, there is no other side to a crisis that did not begin but only accelerated in 2020. Any sufficient performance studies for after the end of this world must grapple with that fact.

Each year, as if on cue, my students rediscover the irony that "the body" that is centered in performance studies is itself an abstract concept that threatens to alienate them from the lived experience of their bodies. Sometimes, the discovery of this irony is intensified into a paranoid rejection of "theory" as the culprit behind the appearance of all such abstractions in the curriculum and in their lives. Certainly, when theory is presented in its most arborescent form—a vertical tree of knowledge that each supplicant must arduously climb—then it might certainly deserve such dismissal. But when thought along the horizontal axis spreads—not a tree but a viney undergrowth—then the more anarchic possibilities of theory might be released back into the wild.[7] This is to say, putting Emma Goldman in the affirmative, that if I *can* dance, then I *want* to be in your revolution. This is also to say, with Saidiya Hartman, that the fugitive movements of the wayward can amount to "the mutual aid offered up in the open-air prison," can figure as a "queer resource of black survival."[8]

I'm happy to have this toolkit of theory and practice to share and learn from in the uncertain days ahead. I hope you will too.

Notes

1 José Esteban Muñoz, *Cruising Utopia: The Then and There of Queer Futurity* (New York: New York University Press, 2009).

2 Sylvia Wynter, "Unsettling the Coloniality of Being/Power/Truth/Freedom: Towards the Human, After Man, Its Overrepresentation—An Argument," *CR: The New Centennial Review* 3, no. 3 (2003): 257–337.

3 Jacqueline Shea Murphy, *The People Have Never Stopped Dancing: Native American Modern Dance Histories* (Minneapolis: University of Minnesota Press, n.d.).

4 Mark Fisher, *Capitalist Realism: Is There No Alternative?* (Washington, DC: O Books, 2009).

5 André Lepecki, "Choreography as Apparatus of Capture," *TDR/The Drama Review* 51, no. 2 (2007): 119–23. https://doi.org/10.1162/dram.2007.51.2.119.

6 Jayna Brown, "Buzz and Rumble: Global Pop Music and Utopian Impulse," *Social Text* 28, no. 1–102 (March 1, 2010): 125–46. https://doi.org/10.1215/01642472-2009-063.

7 Jack Halberstam and Tavia Nyong'o, "Theory in the Wild," *SAQ* 117, no. 3 (n.d.): 453–64.

8 Saidiya Hartman, *Wayward Lives, Beautiful Experiments: Intimate Histories of Social Upheaval* (New York and London: Norton, 2019), 228.

OPENING THOUGHTS AND INTRODUCTIONS

Katerina Paramana and Anita Gonzalez

Part 1: From the Edge

Katerina Paramana

It feels as though I am writing this from the edge of a cliff—like Wile E. Coyote, who is already suspended mid-air but does not realize it. Mid-air last thoughts, last wishes, last thank-yous, last goodbyes to the world as we know it: "bye, byeeeeeee!" The first months of 2020 constitute an important moment in history: as a result of Covid-19, there has been an extraordinary level of uncertainty about the future—and about where we will land in just a few months' time. This book's aims and aspirations (from its early stages of conceptualization in 2016 to the conclusion of its writing in the midst of a global pandemic) are immediately connected to our present experiences and looming ends: ends that many have desired for a long time but which do not seem to be coming fast enough (such as the end of capitalism and ensuing capitalist exploitation, white supremacy, and racism); and others we have always dreaded but are coming toward us at high speed (such as the environmental catastrophe). Irrespective of our desires, it feels as though the world—at least the world as we know it—is ending. Capturing the importance, gravity, and potential of the current moment in this opening, especially when there is still so much uncertainty about how things will develop in the next few months, feels like an insurmountable task. Productively addressing the ends that are looming and the manner in which the conversations in this book can contribute to this moment, as well as to the future we are assuming will exist, feels equally difficult. I have agonized over writing this opening text because it feels as though I am writing from the end of this world. The ends are nevertheless nearing.

At the time of writing (Summer 2020), the world is dealing with a series of problems. I will refer to some I feel I can speak to due to my geographical location and experiences. The coronavirus pandemic[1] has not yet been contained due to the prioritization, at least in the UK where I reside, of the economy. In addition, environmental catastrophe is looming—it has been suggested that we are well on our way to returning to pre-lockdown levels of climate crisis.[2] Following the onset of the pandemic, the police killings of George Floyd, Breonna Taylor, Ahmaud Arbery, Tony McDade, and Rayshard Brooks in the United States have unleashed sustained protests against police brutality, white supremacy, and anti-blackness across the world, including mass demonstrations and the tearing down and removal of statues of enslavers and colonizers.[3] Due to economic and social inequalities, Black and Global Majority people everywhere are disproportionately affected by Covid-19 and economic recession. The pandemic is also being used to justify job losses, for many governments are hesitant to financially support workers, institutions, and businesses, in contrast to the bank bailouts of 2008. In India, for example, millions of migrant workers have lost their employment and had to return to their villages, many of them on foot. In the United Kingdom and the United States, both the academic[4] and the arts[5] worlds are imploding due to insufficient state support. Freelance artists are the most affected in the arts, while in academia the pandemic is being used to justify redundancies, precarity, and increased workloads. In Greece, where I was born and raised, the right-wing government is not only failing to acknowledge the needs of culture workers in a Covid-19 world but also recently decided to remove, among others, arts-, social-studies-, and environment-related classes from most secondary education, establishing a politically conservative curriculum.[6]

This pantheon of problems—health, environment, human rights, inequalities, racism, resurgence of fascism, and an increase in conservative politics and policies in many countries—has its roots in the capitalist world before the pandemic. It has its roots in the capitalist political economy. The pandemic has allowed this to become fully visible because it applied enough pressure to the (capitalist political and economic) system to force it to reveal that it was built on fallacies, social and economic inequalities, and problematic ethics intended to satisfy the political interests of those already in power. It is this intersection of politics, economics, and, I suggest, ethics—and the effects of their specific interrelation—that the term "political economy" makes visible and which is therefore used in this book (as opposed to, for example, simply neoliberal capitalism).

Although there are many negative ends looming, if we handle the situation right, perhaps some of the positive ends—the end to capitalism as the current political economic model, for example—can lead to better beginnings. As Arundhati Roy eloquently put it,

> Historically, pandemics have forced humans to break with the past and imagine their world anew. This one is no different. It is a portal, a gateway between one world and the next.
> We can choose to walk through it, dragging the carcasses of our prejudice and hatred, our avarice, our data banks and dead ideas, our dead rivers and smoky skies behind us. Or we can walk through lightly, with little luggage, ready to imagine another world. And ready to fight for it.[7]

There are signs that we might be moving in a positive direction. The demonstrations across the world against the environmental crisis, police brutality, racism, and deep-rooted inequalities, as well as the political involvement of both Millennials and Zoomers, are all good signs (the latter recently managed to keep the stadium of Trump's June 20, 2020 rally in Tulsa almost empty by reserving tickets so that it appeared sold out[8]). Furthermore, the relationship between racism and the political economy of capitalism (the latter's engendering of the former, for it was the enslaved that provided the original capital[9]) has entered popular discourse and consciousness. Interviews given on national channels by central figures such as Angela Davis and Cornel West, and made available on social media platforms like YouTube, were instrumental to this.[10] In the UK, and as a result of petitions during the pandemic, there is now a government consultation for the possibility of Universal Basic Income.[11] Petitions are also circulating in the UK for the teaching of colonial history in schools and pressures are being put to universities for the decolonization of the curriculum and to address racism in their power structures. Previously unthinkable, suggestions for the defunding of the police and for investment instead in communities are now being implemented in some US states. People are engaging. Protests, mutual aid groups, petitions, community organizing—all are positive signs of a desire and initiation of action for change at a global level.[12] There is a bodily visceral reaction to what is happening. The more our hands and feet feel tied due to the physical restrictions imposed by the pandemic and we are prevented from touching others, the more we seem to want to reach out through different types of solidarity. We perhaps finally realize we are not individuals nor nations, but interdependent and therefore relying on each other for care, safety, love, and prosperity. The imposed slowdown of life as a result of the pandemic has forced us to rethink, reprioritize, listen with our bodies, and act with them. This is what this book is about: the relation of our bodies to those things that seem so far and separate from them but are in fact immediately connected; for bodies and political economies affect one another at both the micro and macro levels.[13] This book then stands in the space between ends and beginnings, and reimagines what a world can be like through a dialogue between performance, dance, and political economy.

Part 2: On Rage

Anita Gonzalez

We could be at the end of the world as we have known it. The performance economy shifts perceptibly, perhaps irretrievably as we watch a deluge of global economies crashing around our bodies. The threads of capitalism and the overcharged activities of neoliberalism have paused for a brief moment. Some have responded to this moment with thoughtful reflection. Others— on both sides of the political spectrum—respond with rage to infringement upon human liberties. In this temporal moment of Summer 2020, Black Lives Matter protests expose centuries of injustices against African diaspora people. At the same time, in Michigan, where I live, citizens accustomed to unencumbered freedom rebel against the confinement of medical masks which they claim muzzle breath and limit speech. Armed protestors have repeatedly stormed the state capital in response to a mandate from the governor for residents to wear masks.[14] Within the eye of this social and economic hurricane all types of protestors gather calling for change. Artists and scholars are responding to the disrupted order. Quarantined at home, distant from familiar desks, studios, or theaters, many have reassessed their privileged perspectives. Each of us has recognized the fragility of our lives and personal economies. Collectively the pandemic of Covid-19 has made artists casualties of a capitalist production machine for the arts which grinds to a halt. Rage is one phoenix rising from the silence of this stalled economic machine.

Tonya Pinkins, a Tony award-winning actress, writes in an online blog:

> 2020 gifted us the perfect storm to herald the winds of societal change. . . . The American theater has been dying a slow death from its racist, nostalgic, blacklisting and anglophilia on top of its soon to be extinct subscription audience. It has flatlined and debating whether there will be a Lazarus resurrection in 2022 seems so frivolous to me while young men and women are shot with rubber bullets, Black men are being lynched from trees and Americans are being brutalized by the Police who are sworn to serve and protect their constitutional right to free speech.[15]

However, this stopping of the economic machine is not really a solution, for stresses on the global economy have only intensified inequalities. They have underscored the continuing and continual disenfranchisement of those most at risk. Katerina Paramana details the types of social problems exacerbated by the pandemic. Service workers, health practitioners, and BIPOC individuals (Black, Indigenous, and People of Color) have borne the brunt of business closures and unemployment. Yet artistry persists. While activists throughout the world have seized the moment to protest in the streets for the humanity of Black lives, artists in the United States have rejected normalized structures of art-making by insisting upon institutional restructuring of arts organizations. There are many examples. The *We See You* campaign,[16] initiated by a coalition of 3,000 artists and co-signed by 50,000 US artists, published a manifesto demanding overdue change and a sweeping new social contract for the American theater. Equitable presence, codes of conduct, and transformative practices are central to these demands. The manifesto builds upon an earlier (2016) statement by playwright August Wilson called "The Ground on Which I Stand" about unequal funding for Black arts.[17] Both manifestos describe a need to destabilize underpinnings of hierarchical economies in order to shake loose new methodologies for imagining redistribution of resources.

Perhaps the practice of art has already enabled artists in several disciplines to imagine alternatives to hierarchical models. Embodied performance and dance practices in particular reimagine social structures by modeling alternative collaborative behaviors. When Black and other bodies engage in collective exchanges of kinaesthetic energy they represent more equitable structures of human interactions; they offer hope. Because I am not a scientist, I'm not sure how brain synapses react in the rehearsal studio when physical forms engage in collective actions. I'm not sure how physical or mental mechanisms mobilize in distressed bodies to resist material systems that contribute to their dis-ease. But, I do believe in art as a potential palliative to physical and social distress.

When Katerina and I began conversations about this book in 2018, we imagined it as a scholarly investigation of intersections between political economies and embodiment or dance. Our intent was always to consider contemporary performance in light of politico-economic impacts on society and on dance and performance practices. The global circulation of Covid-19 changed our perceptions about how this book might be received by the scholarly and artistic community. At the same time, issues at the core of our planned conversation have become even more relevant. Since the time when we first contacted our contributors in 2019, life within the contemporary capitalist political economy has become even more precarious. Its negative impact on performance communities is undeniable. However, performing arts are resilient. For example, even without touching, even in isolation, artists dance in the streets, in their bedrooms, through their computers, from their Zoom rooms. They seek embodied communal communication with one another. Our contributing authors have gestured toward this understanding in their writings as they acknowledge the pertinent potency of mutual aid, gravity, community, and experimentation inherent in dance practices. This moment, which might feel like the end of the world, carries embers of hope for a reorientation of political economics through the arts.

Part 3: Introductions

Katerina Paramana and Anita Gonzalez

This book examines the relation between bodies (through the prism of performance and dance, in its expanded sense to include the body, embodiment, and the choreographic) and political economy. We are interested in the critique and insights they can offer to one another and the affordances of this dialogical exchange. Our primary questions are: What can the discourse and practice of performance/dance contribute to contemporary political economy and to its critique? What can current thinking and conversations within the field of political economy contribute to conversations on performance/dance, its role and currency within contemporary political economies, and its futurity? And, ultimately, what new insights can the examination of the relation between performance/dance and political economy offer that can contribute to imagining a world beyond the present? These are the questions to which we invited the contributors of this book to respond, addressing them from their (inter)disciplinary perspective and areas of interest or research.

The experimental approach, format, and structure of this book separate it from a conventional full-length edited collection. For example, as the title of this chapter suggests, the book does not offer a conventional introduction. Although it offers elements of both a preface (e.g., it begins by discussing how and why the book came into being) and of an introduction (it discusses the context, motivations, rationale, questions, process of writing, and structure of this book), the theoretical framework and its relation to other texts interrogating similar concerns is offered instead in Katerina Paramana's provocation chapter "Performance, Dance and Political Economy: A Provocation," which initiated the conversation with co-editor Anita Gonzalez and our contributing authors. We did not displace that material in order to include it here, because we wanted to stay faithful to that conversation and its temporality. Furthermore, as already alluded to, the book is a result of conversations with scholars and artists across disciplines who are interested in the intersection of political economy and arts. We are therefore not working from within dance and performance studies (speaking only to dance and performance scholars), but we instead begin the conversation from the in-between relationship of the fields. Our contributors, selected for their expertise and unique point of entry into our topic, are Marc Arthur, Melissa Blanco Borelli, Alexandrina Hemsley, Jamila Johnson-Small, and Tavia Nyong'o from performance/dance studies, and Elena Loizidou, Nina Power, and Usva Seregina from political theory, social theory, and economics/consumer culture, respectively. Although currently all find themselves in the United States and the United Kingdom, we all bring different personal, cultural, and socioeconomic histories and many have lived for many years in other countries such as Cyprus, Finland, Russia, and Greece. We therefore hope that our histories bring multiple perspectives and insights into the writing of this book. Lastly, unlike a conventional edited collection, this is a short book of different kinds of writing (both academic essays and performative texts, offering different kinds insights) by scholars and artists from different disciplines, which arose from live dialogical exchanges with them.

The aforementioned scholars and artists were invited to contribute to the project with two online conversations and two short texts arising from them (a 3,000-word essay and a 2,000-word text). We asked each contributor to participate in a preliminary twenty to thirty minutes informal online conversation with us (Paramana and Gonzalez) to establish a common ground, perhaps also vocabulary, answer any questions, and consider their interests, potential approach to the terms "performance/dance" and "political economy," and their way in and contribution to the project. This conversation also allowed us to co-produce a viewing playlist of short videos of events/performances: we asked each of our contributors to email us with links to video examples that in their opinion dealt with the intersection of performance/dance and political economy. We then invited them to respond via an essay or performative text to two or more videos in the playlist. Their selection of videos for their response was based on their own aesthetics and interests. The playlist, varied in its selection, included the following videos:

The Video Playlist (approx. seventy-one minutes)

1. Trailer for Paul Wright's *Arcadia* (2018) https://www.youtube.com/watch?v=iyrA4uO9VsI
2. *Acid Corbynism*: https://twitter.com/ashcowburn/status/912449218568220672?lang=en

   (**Note** re: *Acid Corbynism: https://www.redpepper.org.uk/what-is-acid-corbynism/*)
3. Taisha Paggett, *I Believe in Echoes* (2018) https://www.youtube.com/watch?v=pRWbjtcya7E
4. Merce Cunningham, *Exchange* (2018) https://youtu.be/ciBqm_XtYVE
5. From 2:26–9:09 minutes: Regina José Galindo, *Tierra* (2013) https://youtu.be/RdCdZnVB6bw
6. Wangechi Mutu + Santigold, *The End of Eating Everything* (2013) https://youtube.com/watch?v=wMZSCfqOxVs
7. nibia pastrana santiago (Puerto Rico), *danza actual o el evento coreografico . . .* (2015) https://vimeo.com/154271141
8. The Blaze music video for "Territory" (French group) (2017) https://www.youtube.com/watch?v=54fea7wuV6s
9. Jonathan Gonzalez, *Handwritten Notes* (2016) https://www.youtube.com/watch?v=Nz0XDhVFpJA
10. Christian Falsnaes, *FORCE* (2018) (documentation excerpts)

    (The performance involves a bunch of headphones that are given to audience members and they are to follow the instructions given): https://youtu.be/n-lwoBlGdkY

11. Ebony Noelle Golden's *125th and Freedom: Public Performance Ritual* (2017) (highlight reel): https://www.youtube.com/watch?v=-rXPt2wHzoE

12. Becky Edmund's film, *Goodbye Love* (2015) https://vimeo.com/151298203

13. From 5–6 minutes and 15:50–21 minutes (watch all if you can!): Bojana Cvejić and Christine de Smedt, *Spatial Confessions* (2014) https://www.youtube.com/watch?v=_PEDcLVVUdc

14. Cotton bullet collective, *Metsä²* (I couldn't find a video, but their blog, which is both in Finnish and in English, has decent descriptions and photo documentation): https://cottonbulletcollective.com/works/

15. Jeremy Deller's recent film about rave, *Everybody in The Place: An Incomplete History of Britain 1984–1992* (2018) https://vimeo.com/278494935

16. ACT UP & ACT NOW Seize control of the FDA October 11, 1988. (Please choose and focus on an excerpt of maximum 9 minutes) https://www.youtube.com/watch?v=s70aCOflRgY&t=817s

The essay responses to these videos were another way the contributors engaged with the book's concerns. It also afforded them the opportunity to engage with one another for the first time. In addition to this dialogical exchange, we invited them to respond to two provocation texts by the editors. Inviting responses to both videos (co-produced playlist) and texts (editors' provocations) was important because of the different kinds of insights the different modalities would offer.

The fourth dialogical exchange was a second live conversation, this time among all contributors. The group conversation involved responses to one another's writing within dialogical pairings—within "Dialogues"—as well as wider group discussion. The pairings, consisting of varying combinations of essay responses to videos and essay responses to provocations, were based upon core ideas emerging from the essays which could dialogue in a fruitful manner with one another. The pairings resulted in six Dialogues. Lastly, Tavia Nyong'o contributed to the four dialogical exchanges by responding to them with the Foreword to this book.

The book's structure and format reflect the dialogical nature and the timeline of the project. The editors' provocations, which initiate the discussion, are followed by the six Dialogues, which are choreographed into the book. The book closes with an edited transcript of the group conversation.

The group conversation expanded on and extended key concerns explored in the chapters about the relation between bodies and political economy (such as rest, productivity, rage, resistance, survival, control, commodification, inequalities, care, mutual aid, anarchism, community, *convivencia*, and ideological endings). This led to discussion about the necessity for a new configuration of our bodies to political economy and the environment; a reconfiguration that has been necessary for quite some time and is now demanded by the pandemic. What became evident through our thinking of different configurations, different structures, different choreographies, is the importance of rhythm, trust, and working together, and of performance improvisation training. Listening not only with our ears but with our bodies and senses, and listening intently to one another and to the current situation as a result of the pandemic, was articulated as crucial to changing the relation of our bodies to political economy. Perhaps for that very reason, continuing to examine the relation between political economy (where politics, economics, and ethics intersect and the specific ways they do so in contemporary capitalism) and bodies (though the prism of performance and dance and the skills they offer) can continue to offer insights into the new configurations needed. *Performance, Dance and Political Economy: Bodies at the End of the World*, through a critical exploration of this relation, offers some insights for imagining and materializing a world beyond the present.

Notes

1 Many have attributed the pandemic to environmental degradation: Damian Carrington, "Pandemics Result from Destruction of Nature, Say UN and WHO," *The Guardian*, June 17, 2020. https://www.theguardian.com/world/2020/jun/17/pandemics-destruction-nature-un-who-legislation-trade-green-recovery

2 Fiona Harvey, "World Has Six Months to Avert Climate Crisis, Says Energy Expert," *The Guardian*, June 18, 2020. Available online: https://www.theguardian.com/environment/2020/jun/18/world-has-six-months-to-avert-climate-crisis-says-energy-expert

3 See, for example, articles about institutional racism in the police in the UK and about the removal of statues in the UK:
- https://www.theguardian.com/uk-news/2020/aug/09/system-needs-to-change-dawn-butler-on-being-stopped-by-police

- https://www.theguardian.com/uk-news/2020/jun/07/blm-protesters-topple-statue-of-bristol-slave-trader-edward-colston

4 Amelia Horgan, "The Universities Crisis Is the Moment to End a Decade of Marketisation," *NewStatesman*, June 25, 2020. https://www.newstatesman.com/politics/education/2020/06/universities-crisis-moment-end-decade-marketisation.

5 Clara Palliard, "Emergency Funding for Culture Now," Website campaign. https://you.38degrees.org.uk/petitions/emergency-funding-for-culture-now?fbclid=IwAR1pwafUlGj39O9Jn3-Hf3Lo526ysYvZTSUgFToSpLSsu9cYs1FB4P0m3G4.

6 Avaaz.org Petition, "No to the Abolition of Art Classes." Created June 17, 2020. https://secure.avaaz.org/community_petitions/el/ypoyrgos_paideias_niki_kerameos_ohi_stin_katargisi_ton_kallitehnikon_mathimaton/?fIILikb&fbclid=IwAR1M4Y8Esux6BJX67JfW2SegbgZUq1nR2qwAVJHD_YhnPdGMYwsqHcSafk. And "SYRIZA Goes to the Parliament Against the Decision to Abolish Arts Classes," *Ee Avgi*, June 19, 2020.

7 Arundhati Roy, "The Pandemic Is a Portal," *Financial Times*, April 3, 2020 (from her forthcoming Haymarket Books publication *Azadi: Freedom. Fascism. Fiction*). https://www.ft.com/content/10d8f5e8-74eb-11ea-95fe-fcd274e920ca.

8 Maggie Haberman and Annie Karni, "The President's Shock at the Empty Rows of Seats at Tulsa," *The New York Times,* June 21, 2020. https://www.nytimes.com/2020/06/21/us/politics/trump-tulsa-rally.html. https://www.nytimes.com/2020/06/21/us/politics/trump-tulsa-rally.html.

9 Cedric J. Robinson, *Black Marxism: The Making of the Black Radical Tradition* (Chapel Hill: University of North Carolina Press, 2000 [1983]).

10 *Democracy Now*. Interview with Angela Davis, "We Can't Eradicate Racism Without Eradicating Racial Capitalism," YouTube video June 14, 2020. https://www.youtube.com/watch?v=qhh3CMkngkY&feature=share&fbc...IwAR1nX0Z_-tsxz-jz7uu3fP4xKwPjeomLurPKflSIwDl26w_y7p-zFI_zLmgs; and *Democracy Now*. "America's Moment of Reckoning: Cornel West Says National Uprising Is a Sign of Empire Imploding," Interview of Cornel West with Nermeen Shaikh, June 1, 2020. https://www.democracynow.org/2020/6/1/cornel_west_us_moment_of_reckoning?fbclid=IwAR3ImsxibsSKG2O2cgbjL4YSnHT47LBL3e7gIjIMMGhECUv3HY8PNqcHBMo.

11 Universal Basic Income: https://www.organise.org.uk/blog/2020/6/12/universal-basic-income-this-is-our-chance?rq=Universal%20Basic%20income.

12 Franco Berardi Bifo refers to current mobilizations as "an insurrection of precarious workers who are black, white, Latino, and especially young, although not only young . . . . This is a real social insurrection against racism and against capitalism." (Deja Crnovic, "Franco Berardi Bifo: Permanent Insurrection Is the Only Way to Breathe," *Disenz*, June 22, 2020. https://www.disenz.net/en/franco-berardi-bifo-permanent-insurrection-is-the-only-way-to-breathe/.)

13 Slavoj Žižek suggests that "Globalization today shouldn't mean abolishing quarantines" but it should instead "mean tightly coordinating procedures and helping each other. That's the life-and-death question: Will we be able as humanity to coordinate our resources in order to confront together what looms ahead, or will this logic of bubbles continue to predominate?" (Jonathan Jacobson, "Slavoj Žižek's 'Brutal, Dark' Formula for Saving the World," *HAARETZ.com*. June 4, 2020. https://www.haaretz.com/misc/article-print-page/.premium.MAGAZINE-slavoj-zizek-s-brutal-dark-formula-to-save-the-world-1.8898051). David Harvey agrees and asks that we seriously consider how to proceed: "Why don't we come out of this crisis by creating an entirely different kind of social order? Why don't we take those elements with which the current collapsing bourgeois society is pregnant—its astonishing science and technology and productive capacity—and liberate them, making use of artificial intelligence and technological change and organizational forms so that we can actually create something radically different than anything that existed before? After all, in the midst of this emergency, we are already experimenting with alternative systems of all sorts, from the free supply of basic foods to poor neighborhoods and groups, to free medical treatments, alternative access structures through the internet, and so on. In fact, the lineaments of a new socialist society are already being laid bare—which is probably why the right wing and the capitalist class are so anxious to get us back to the status quo ante. This is a moment of opportunity to think through what an alternative might look like." (David Harvey, "David Harvey: We Need a Collective Response to the Collective Dilemma of Coronavirus," *Jacobin*, April 24, 2020. Available online: https://www.jacobinmag.com/2020/04/david-harvey-coronavirus-pandemic-capital-economy).

14 Meagan Flynn, "Chanting 'Lock Her Up,' Michigan Protesters Waving Trump Flags Mass Against Gov. Gretchen Whitmer's Coronavirum Restrictions," *The Washington Post*, April 16, 2020. Available online: https://www.washingtonpost.com/nation/2020/04/16/michigan-whitmer-conservatives-protest/.

15 Tonya Pinkins, "Why I Am Fed Up with Performative Activism from White and Black Theatre Makers," *Medium.com*, July 10, 2020. Available online: https://medium.com/@tonyapinkins/why-i-am-fed-up-with-performative-activism-from-white-and-black-theater-makers-d46564ec94fe.

16 *We See You* (https://www.weseeyouwat.com/).

17 August Wilson, "The Ground on Which I Stand," *American Theatre*, June 20, 2016. Available online: https://www.americantheatre.org/2016/06/20/the-ground-on-which-i-stand/. This is a reprint of a speech delivered by playwright August Wilson on June 26, 1996.

PROVOCATIONS

Provocation 1

1 PERFORMANCE, DANCE AND POLITICAL ECONOMY
A PROVOCATION
Katerina Paramana

This text is a provocation addressed to my fellow co-editor, Anita Gonzalez, and to our contributing authors. It sought to initiate our discussion about the relationship between bodies (through the prism of performance and dance) and political economy, articulate the importance of these terms and the increasing significance of their interrelation, and pose the questions to which we invited the contributors to respond.

* * *

Bodies and Political Economy

The relationship between politics, economics, and ethics in a society affects not only how just that society is, but also its citizens' experience of *eudaimonia* (i.e., of welfare, flourishing, prosperity, and feeling of happiness). In the Classical Ancient Greek categorization of spheres of knowledge, *economy* was subordinated to *politics* and *ethics* (i.e., political and ethical concerns were considered more important and therefore economic decisions depended on them), and human's *eudaimonia* could only be conceptualized in relation to justice in the *polis*.[1] Today, the experience has been reversed: *politics* and *ethics* are subordinated to *economy*,[2] for neoliberal capitalism considers everything, including social relations, in economic terms.[3] It marketizes all areas of life, transforming people into economic subjects that need to be self-interested competitors,[4] and demands entrepreneurialism and constant productivity. In doing so, Kathi Weeks suggests, it reduces our needs and passions to only work and acquisition, making "workers out of human beings," impoverishing our senses, and diminishing our "affective capacities and modes of sociality."[5] The neoliberal capitalist configuration of the three spheres of knowledge, then, has affected the relationship between self, others, time, space, and the environment and has led to the exacerbation of inequality, as well as to precarity, unmanageable workloads, injustice, and environmental destruction. The contemporary subject, therefore, experiences ever-increasing feelings of alienation, anxiety, and melancholia;[6] the possibility for *eudaimonia* is being indefinitely postponed.

In this text, I discuss why looking at the relationship between bodies (through the prism of dance and performance) and political economy is important and how it might help us reconfigure the current relationship of politics and ethics to economy. To do so, I first address the terms political economy and dance (broadly conceived), emphasizing the importance of their specific interrelation. I then situate the concerns of this book in relation to other texts with similar concerns. I end by pointing to the increasing significance of closely examining the relation between bodies and political economy if we are to imagine a world beyond the present, and open the conversation to you (my co-editor, Anita Gonzalez, and our contributing authors).

The subsumption of everything by economy has been arguably aided by the artificial separation of the study of politics and economics that began with the publication of neoclassical economist Alfred Marshall's *Principles of Economics* in 1890.[7] From then until the late twentieth century, political economy as a distinct field was replaced by the separate disciplines of sociology, economics, political science, and international relations. Marshall separated his area of expertise (economics) from political economy, privileging the former.[8] Political economy was revived in the second half of the twentieth century "to provide a broader framework for understanding complex national and international problems and events."[9] Today, as a *field*, political economy includes the study of "the politics of economic relations, domestic political and economic issues, the comparative study of political and economic systems, and international political economy" and is therefore considered a "holistic study of individuals, states, markets, and society."[10] This is a critical point because, although the *field* of political economy recognizes and examines the interrelation of politics and economics, what we instead often observe *in practice* is that economic solutions, despite stemming from political decisions based on political interests, are instead presented as if they are objective data based on mathematical necessity (and therefore as irrefutable). Consider, for example, the financial crises that several European Union countries have faced since 2009 and the "solutions" (in the form of austerity measures) that have been imposed on them, irrespective of the catastrophic effects it is clear they produce. What kinds of politics and, equally importantly, ethics are these decisions based on?

Political economy (that of, for example, neoliberal capitalism) is where politics, economics, and, I suggest, ethics intersect most visibly, because every economic decision is both a political and an ethical decision as well. The term therefore affords the opportunity to point to the intersection of politics, economics, and ethics and the effects of their specific interrelation. It is for this reason that it is used in this book, as opposed to simply capitalism.

The misconception or misrepresentation of the extent to which politics and economics are intertwined—or their conscious and deliberate separation—is, in my experience, often also reflected in the lack of conversations in the United States and the United Kingdom about class, its relation to race, gender, sexuality, ethnicity, location, ability, and age, and, therefore, its relation to power, wealth, and poverty. It is also often manifested in the lack of awareness of the manner in which individuals and groups are embedded in specific political economies and are, or can be, complicit or resistant to them through their actions and practices. The election of Trump in the United States and the Brexit referendum in the United Kingdom have brought discussions of class back into conversation.[11] In the academic and professional performance and especially dance worlds, however, although identity politics are examined, they are often not accompanied by conversations about our relation, as citizens, academics, and artists, to political economy and class. The level of prominence of these conversations in the dance world varies in different environments and geographical locations, but they seem to occur more frequently among oppressed groups, which tend to be more politically conscious.[12] However, as I will shortly elaborate, dance offers important insights into the contemporary capitalist political economy and to its critique.

Dance, understood in this book in an expanded manner to include the body, embodiment, and the choreographic, as a field of scholarly and artistic practice, is undoubtebly affected by and affects the economies of which it is a part. Furthermore, contemporary dance is an economy itself: one that is contested and ill-defined and where financial, institutional, and ideological interests interact as the "field" of "contemporary" dance.[13] Elsewhere, I have argued that the field's advancement is the UK is prevented due to its relation to the contemporary political economy: the dance world often reproduces neoliberal forms of conduct.[14] However, I suggested that dance offers important insights into the body and its relation to others and to the environment that are especially important in the contemporary moment. I proposed this is because:

> Dance is very skilled at "seeing" time and space and the relationship of the body to them, at finding ways to negotiate, organise, create and break rules, find joy in being in the same space and time with others, working with others, understanding the body—its mechanics, flow, experience and relation to other bodies—and listening to [it], its rhythms and needs.[15]

These skills and insights are especially important in contemporary capitalism, in which "[o]ur bodies feel acutely the terrible tension between the rhythms imposed by the outside world—a world 'of fear, competition and precariousness'[16]—and those necessitated by their own needs and desires."[17] As Stefano Harney and Fred Moten observe, capitalism has also led to a pervasive soullessness in our working practices, the choreography of our everyday life's decision-making and activities, and to feelings of disembodiedness and melancholia.[18] Therefore, the examination of the relation between political economy and bodies, specifically through the prism of performance and dance, and the exploration of the potential that emerges from it are critical. It is this relation this short book explores.

Some Specifics

Conversations about work, labor, and class, as well as the latter's intersections with, for example, race and gender will be important to this conversation. It is also necessary to clarify that the term "class" is primarily being used to refer to groups of people who have the same socioeconomic status and that class is considered to determine (to a great extent) one's political and ideological consciousness.[19] In other words, we are primarily drawing from Marxist class-theory, which proposes a class-based analysis of political economy and points to conflicts that are inherent in a society's organization and the resultant intersection of capital and market.[20] At the same time, Foucault's critique of capitalism, which emphasizes the organizational aspects of capital and the identification of managers as rulers, is essential to the conversation here as it highlights the relation of class struggle to a critique of neoliberal capitalism.[21] Furthermore, this conversation takes into consideration Bernard Stiegler's distinction between the proletariat and the working class, identifying the former with what he refers to as today's *"proletarianized consumer"*: one whose knowledge and attention, and, as a result, libidinal energy has been harnessed and exploited.[22] Lastly, in order to understand how class impacts one's actions, it is important to make clear that what is being referred to by "class interests" is a range of issues such as standards of living, working conditions, leisure, level of toil, and material security.[23]

Looking Back

Although much has been written about the relationship between performance/dance and politics,[24] the relation between performance/dance and political economy that this book examines has not been addressed to the same extent nor explored in the interdisciplinary and dialogical manner pursued here. This book brings into dialogue political theorists, dance and performance theorists and artists, social theorists, and economists/consumer culture theorists and draws from the fields of dance, performance, theater, and political economy. The following is a review of texts with similar concerns to this book from these fields.

In dance studies, most texts that have addressed political economy are articles or chapters and therefore are limited in scope.[25] Work that addresses political economy as it relates to dance *as a field* is found in one book chapter and two journal issues. Jane Desmond's 2017 chapter "Tracking the Political Economy of Dance" in *The Oxford Handbook of Dance and Politics* addresses political economy, however its main interest lies in problematizing "processes of transporting community-based dance practices to the stage."[26] The two journal issues, both entitled "Dancing Economies," are the 2009 issue of *Conversations Across the Field of Dance Studies*, edited by Vida Midgelow, and the 2017 *Dance Research* journal issue edited by Lise Uytterhoeven and Melissa Blanco Borelli—my article in the latter, titled "The Contemporary Dance Economy: Problems and Potentials in the Contemporary Neoliberal Moment," is the seed for this book.[27] Dance studies books relevant to the discussion here due to the significance of their insights into the relationship of dance to politics are, for example, Alexandra Kolb's edited collection *Dance and Politics* (2011) and Stacey Prickett's *Embodied Politics: Dance, Protest and Identities* (2013).[28] The former examines the intersection of dance and political studies, while the latter analyzes dance through the lenses of politics, hegemony, and cultural representation. Randy Martin, through his body of work, has brought into conversation economy, polity, and culture via the all-pervasive derivative logic.[29] Connecting finance (the movement of capital) to the history of dance, he demonstrates how the financial market logic informs social values and consequently affects cultural production.[30] Stefan Hölscher's and Gerald Siegmund's edited volume *Dance, Politics & Co-Immunity* (2013) explores dances' relation to the political, making connections between politics, dance, community, and globalization.[31] Furthermore, Ramsay Burt, in *Ungoverning Dance: Contemporary European Theatre Dance and the Commons* (2017), examines dance works since the mid-1990s in relation to post-fordism and neoliberalism. Interested in their effects on dance and dancers, he discusses them in terms of concepts such as virtuosity, responsibility, ethics of relationality, history, and memory.[32] Most recently, from dance and sociological perspectives and with a focus on Brussels and Berlin, Annelies Van Assche's *Labor and Aesthetics in European Contemporary Dance: Dancing Precarity* (2020) examines precarity in the European contemporary dance sector and the effects of working and living conditions on the artistic work's process and outcomes.[33]

Important performance studies perspectives for their work on the relationship between performance and politics are, for example, Bojana Kunst's *Artist at Work: Proximity of Art and Capitalism* (2015).[34] Examining contemporary performance works from a philosophical point view, Kunst aims to understand the "ambivalent proximity of art and capitalism" in order to affirm "artistic practice that happens through thinking about the economic and social conditions of the artist's work."[35] In *Regimes of Invisibility in Contemporary Art, Theory and Culture: Image, Racialization, History* (2017), editors Marina Gržinić and Aneta Stojnić, focusing on Europe, revisit theories of new media technology and art to examine global capitalism in relation to biopolitics, (de)coloniality, and questions of migration, class, race, and gender.[36] In their second edited volume, *Shifting Corporealities in Contemporary Performance: Danger, Im/mobility and Politics* (2018), Gržinić and Stojnić investigate corporeality and embodiment in contemporary artistic practices in relation to "contemporary global necro-capitalism." An interdisciplinary volume, it examines the body "as a site of a new meaning-making politics."[37]

There are many texts within theater studies that address the relationship between theater and politics. Influential to the discussion here are, for example, Joe Kelleher's *Theatre & Politics* (2009), which draws on a broad range of philosophical writing and theatrical examples to raise questions about the complex relationship between politics and theater and the assumptions often made about their relation when they inhabit the same (the theatrical) space.[38] Nicholas Ridout's *Passionate Amateurs: Theatre, Communism, and Love* (2013) investigates modern theater and contemporary performance in the United States and Europe. Focusing on questions about the social function of theater in modern capitalism and its political potential, Ridout suggests that theater can aid our rethinking of notions of time, work, and freedom.[39] Alan Read's *The Dark Theatre: A Book About Loss* (2020) is a "call for angry arts advocacy." It suggests that performance is no longer a political remedy but a "a loss adjustor measuring damages suffered, compensations due, wrongs that demand to be put right."[40] Lastly, Michael Shane Boyle's article "Performance and Value: The Work of Theatre in Karl Marx's Critique of Political Economy" (2017) examines the value of theater from a Marxist perspective. He suggests that although theater as an aesthetic activity has political usefulness and often "breaks with the capitalist mode," it nevertheless conforms to the process of capitalist production and performing in it ensures capitalist productivity.[41] The works discussed here offer significant insights into the understanding of the relationship between theater/performance, politics, and economy; however, they are not working in the interdisciplinary and dialogical manner pursued by this book.

There are many texts on political economy. David Harvey's decades-spanning body of work is perhaps the most referenced.[42] Fewer texts have explored the relation between political economy and class. The seminal thinker on political economy and class in relation to art is Pierre Bourdieu. Bourdieu discusses the relation of class to art via a conversation of class, taste, and culture. He understands class differently than Marx—for him, one's class depends on the specific composition of economic and cultural capital she possesses and results in her specific "habitus," which in turn provides the framework for her cultural taste and informs her behaviors.[43] Nevertheless, Bourdieu does not bring dance or performance explicitly into conversation with political economy. With regards to political economy and class, of interest here are Éric Alliez and Maurizio Lazzarato's *Wars and Capital* (2018) and Jacques Bidet's *Foucault with Marx* (2016). *Wars and Capital* proposes a counter-history of capitalism in order to "recover the reality" of wars of race, class, gender, and sex, of civilization and the environment, and "wars of subjectivity . . . that constitute the secret motor of liberal governmentality."[44]

In *Foucault with Marx*, Bidet discusses the close links between class struggle and neoliberalism.[45] He examines Marxist and Foucauldian criticisms of capitalism and presents them as capitalist modernity's two sides. Lastly, in *For a New Critique of Political Economy* (2010), Bernard Stiegler proposes that critiquing political economy as "*commerce* that has become *exchange*" necessitates "aiming at the examination of both economics and politics, and speaking about them insofar as they are *indissociable*."[46] For him the contemporary political economy has resulted in the "*proletarianized consumer*,"[47] weakening fundamentally the Marxist theory of class struggle.[48] Demonstrating this indissociability of politics and economics is of particular interest to this book.

What sets this book apart from the aforementioned dance, performance, theater, and political economy texts is its interdisciplinary perspective, dialogical approach, and examination of the relation of bodies—specifically through the prism of performance and dance—to political economy and class. In addition, the writing in this volume arises from *live* dialogues with the contributing authors and manifests in different modes of articulation (essays and performative writing), which offer different *kinds* of insights into the topics of conversation and make it relevant to different audiences.

Looking Forward

Since 2008, crisis has been normalized, taking different forms across the globe such as the housing market, financial, refugee, and environmental crises. Furthermore, inequality and poverty have been exacerbated to satisfy political interests, while neoliberal capitalism—along with feeding these crises and helping certain groups of people benefit from them while marginalizing others—has fed the reemergence of fascism. It is obvious that we need to imagine a world beyond the present and take sustained action to materialize it. I agree with Slavoj Žižek that we need to look to art and social movements in order to replace the current system with a new one;[49] for art can play a role not only in reminding us that we can change things, but it can imagine new worlds and poke us into action.[50] And performance and dance can offer insights that can help us reimagine and materialize these new worlds.

Along with looking to art and social movements, it is crucial that we embark on a new project of political economy; one that affords us the opportunity to change "our relation to work, transfor[m] our *noetic* processes (processes of perceiving and processing information/thinking), and enhanc[e] our capacity for *being with* others."[51] Kathi Weeks for example suggests that we need nonwork time "to cultivate new needs for pleasures, activities, senses, passions, aspects, and socialities that exceed the options of working and saving, producing and accumulating" and which are "quite different from [the sociality] orchestrated through the capitalist division of labor."[52] Franco Bifo Berardi argues that if working time was reduced and the relation between income and labor was rescinded, if we did away with "the obligation to exchange living-time for survival," then this reduction or unplugging could become "the premise for freely deploying cognitive energies for the benefit of everyone."[53] In the same vein with Berardi, Bernard Stiegler suggests that what needs to change, above all, is our relation to noetic processes.[54] He also proposes that it is crucial that we move away from the current "*economico-political complex of consumption*" and make a social and political investment: "an investment in a common desire, that is, in what Aristotle called *philia*."[55] This investment in *philia*, he argues, can then "form the basis of a new type of economic investment."[56]

In addition to a common desire, what is critical to imagining and materializing a new political economy project is collective action, solidarity among oppressed groups (for identity-oppression is rooted in capitalist dynamics[57] and capitalism engendered racism[58]), and a robust anti-capitalist movement. What new insights can the examination of the relation between bodies (through the prism of performance and dance) and political economy offer that can contribute to this and to a world beyond the present? In our examination of the relation between them, we are interested in the critique and insights they can offer to one another, and the affordances of this dialogical exchange. *What can the discourse and practice of performance/dance contribute to contemporary political economy and to its critique? What can current thinking and conversations within the field of political economy contribute to conversations on performance/dance, its role and currency within contemporary political economies, and its futurity? And (again), ultimately, what new insights can the examination of the relation between performance/dance and political economy offer that can contribute to imagining a world beyond the present? Performance, Dance and Political Economy: Bodies at the End of the World*, through an interdisciplinary, dialogical, critical, and imaginative examination of this relationship, hopes to offer insights for such a world.

Notes

1 Christos P. Baloglou, "The Tradition of Economic Thought in the Mediterranean World from the Ancient Classical Times Through the

Hellenistic Times Until the Byzantine Times and Arab-Islamic World," in Jürgen Georg Backhaus (ed.), *Handbook of History of Economic Thought: Insights on the Founders of Modern Economics* (New York: Springer, 2012), 10–11. This of course seems to ignore the existence of the enslaved and their, and women's, lack of rights.

2 Katerina Paramana, "Re-turning to the Show: Repetition and the Construction of Spaces of Decision, Affect and Creative Possibility," *Performance Research: A Journal of the Performing Arts* 20, no. 5 (2015a): 116–24.

3 Wendy Brown, *Undoing the Demos: Neoliberalism's Stealth Revolution* (New York: Zone Books, 2015).

4 Ibid.

5 Kathi Weeks, "Imagining Non-Work," *Work and Idleness in the Age of the Great Recession*, 2013. Online, https://socialtextjournal.org/periscope_article/imagining-non-work-2/, accessed March 9, 2019.

6 Katerina Paramana, "The Animation of Contemporary Subjectivity in Tino Sehgal's *Ann Lee*," *Performance Research* 24, no. 6 (2019): 114–21.

7 Michael A. Veseth and David N. Balaam, "Political Economy," *Encyclopaedia Britannica*, 2014. Available online: https://www.britannica.com/topic/political-economy.

8 Ibid. This separation of politics and economics is mirrored in the European Union itself, which has never been a political union, because it was built as a financial union only. Agamben argues that the Union is also "illegitimate" because the people never voted for it. See Franco "Bifo" Berardi, "After the European Union," *Verso*, March 16, 2017. Available online: https://www.versobooks.com/blogs/3129-after-the-european-union; Giorgio Agamben, "The Endless Crisis as an Instrument of Power: In Conversation with Giorgio Agamben," *Verso*, June 4, 2013. Available online: https://www.versobooks.com/blogs/1318-the-endless-crisis-as-an-instrument-of-power-in-conversation-with-giorgio-agamben.

9 Ibid.

10 Ibid.

11 Political theorist Jeremy Gilbert and philosopher Franco "Bifo" Berardi have proposed some strategies to face our predicament. See Jeremy Gilbert, "Labour Cannot Ride the Brexit Wave to Socialism, It Must Fight the Nationalist Right," *New Statesman*, February 11, 2019. Available online:

https://www.newstatesman.com/politics/uk/2019/02/labour-cannot-ride-brexit-wave-socialism-it-must-fight-nationalist-right; Berardi, "After the European Union."

12 Part of the problem seems to be the constitution of the field of dance in academic settings (and consequently, since we are talking about an ecology, also professional settings). Although in their co-edited volume *Black Performance Theory*, Thomas F. DeFrantz and my co-editor Anita Gonzalez suggest that "[a]cademic definitions of performance broaden, to recognize affinities and differences among the location and experience of 'black life' in a fragmented, postmodern world," at least in the United States and the United Kingdom, academia itself is still to a great extent, white, female, and middle to upper class, which affects which work and how it is produced, presented, and theorized. Perhaps the constitution of dance academia stems from the required knowledge (and privileging over other genres) of Western dance (ballet and contemporary dance) for entrance into academic programs. This is compounded by the fact that dance lessons for these required genres are primarily accessible only to middle- to upper-class white women, due to both finances and a problematic gendered view of dance. See Thomas F. DeFrantz and Anita Gonzalez, "Introduction: From 'Negro Expression' to 'Black Performance,'" in T. F. DeFrantz and A. Gonzalez (eds.), *Black Performance Theory* (Durham: Duke University Press, 2014).

13 Katerina Paramana, "The Contemporary Dance Economy: Problems and Potentials in the Contemporary Neoliberal Moment," *Dance Research* 35, no. 1 (2017): 75–95.

14 Ibid.

15 Ibid., 91.

16 Franco "Bifo" Berardi, "TedxCalarts: Performance, Body & Presence," *Tedx Online*, March 9, 2013. https://www.new.livestream.com/tedx/tedxcalarts, accessed March 9, 2013.

17 Paramana, "The Animation of Contemporary Subjectivity in Tino Sehgal's *Ann Lee*," 114–21.

18 Stefano Harney and Fred Moten state: "To work today is to be asked, more and more, to do without thinking, to feel without emotion, to move without friction, to adapt without question, to translate without pause, to desire without purpose, to connect without interruption" (Stefano Harney and Fred Moten, *The Undercommons: Fugitive Planning & Black Study* [New York: Minor Compositions, 2013], 87).

19 Pierre Bourdieu, *Distinction: A Social Critique of the Judgement of Taste* (London: Routledge, 1984).

20 Karl Marx, *Capital: A Critique of Political Economy Volume I* (Moscow: Progress Publishers, 1867); Clark Everling, "Marxist Theory: From Class Struggle to Political Economy," in W. J. Samuels (ed.), *Wisconsin "Government and Business" and the History of Heterodox Economic Thought* (Research in the History of Economic Thought and Methodology Series, Volume 22) (Emerald Group Publishing Limited, 2004), 323–45; Veseth and Balaam, "Political Economy"; Jacques Bidet, *Foucault with Marx* (London: Zed Books, 2016); John Milios, "Social Classes in Classical and Marxist Political Economy," *The American Journal of Economics and Sociology* 59, no. 2 (2000): 283–302.

21 Bidet, *Foucault with Marx*.

22 Bernard Stiegler, *For a New Critique of Political Economy* (Cambridge: Polity Press, 2010).

23 Erik Olin Wright (ed.), *Approaches to Class Analysis* (Cambridge: Cambridge University Press, 2005).

24 See, for example, Mark Franko's "Dance and the Political: States of Exception," *Dance Research Journal* 38, no. 1/2 (2006): 3–18; André Lepecki, *Exhausting Dance* (New York: Routledge, 2005); André Lepecki, *Of the Presence of the Body: Essays on Dance and Performance Theory* (Middletown: Wesleyan University Press, 2004).

25 See, for example, articles by: Melissa Blanco Borelli, "Dancing with Žižek: Sublime *Objects* and the Hollywood Dance Film," in B. Chow and Mangold (eds.), *Žižek and Performance. Performance Philosophy* (London: Palgrave Macmillan, 2014); Thomas J. Cottle, "Social Class and Social Dancing," *The Sociological Quarterly* 7, no. 2 (1966): 179–96; Kate Hardy and Teela Sanders, "The Political Economy of 'Lap Dancing': Contested Careers and Women's Work in the Stripping Industry," *Work, Employment, and Society* 29, no. 1 (2014): 119–36; Patricia Sanderson, "The Arts, Social Inclusion and Social Class: The Case of Dance," *British Educational Research Journal* 34 (2008): 467–90; Lito Tsitsou, "Dance, Class and the Body: A Bourdieusian Examination of Training Trajectories into Ballet and Contemporary Dance," *The Scottish Journal of Performance* 1, no. 2 (2014): 63–89 and books by: Ida Meftahi, *Gender and Dance in Modern Iran: Biopolitics on Stage* (Oxon: Routledge, 2016) and Marta Savigliano, *Tango and the Political Economy of Passion: From Exoticism to Decolonization (Institutional Structures of Feeling)* (Boulder: Westview Press, 1995).

26 Jane Desmond, "Tracking the Political Economy of Dance," in R. J. Kowal, G. Siegmund, and R. Martin (eds.), *The Oxford Handbook of Dance and Politics* (New York: Oxford University Press, 2017).

27 Vida Midgelow (ed.), "Dancing Economies," *Conversations Across the Field of Dance Studies* XXIX (2009). Melissa Blanco Borelli and Lise Uytterhoeven (eds.), "Dancing Economies," *Dance Research* 35, no. 1 (2017); Paramana, "The Contemporary Dance Economy," 75–95.

28 Stacey Prickett, *Embodied Politics: Dance, Protest and Identities* (Binsted: Dance Books, 2013); Alexandra Kolb (ed.), *Dance and Politics* (Oxford: Peter Lang, 2011).

29 Randy Martin, *Knowledge LTD: Towards a Social Logic of the Derivative* (Philadelphia: Temple University Press, 2015).

30 Randy Martin, *Dance and Finance—Social Kinesthetics and Derivative Logics*. Public Lecture, EMPAC, NY, 2013. Available online: https://empac.rpi.edu/events/2013/randy-martin; Randy Martin, "A Precarious Dance, a Derivative Sociality," *TDR/The Drama Review* 56, no. 4 (2012): 62–77.

31 Stefan Hölscher and Gerald Siegmund, *Dance, Politics & Co-Immunity* (Chicago: University of Chicago Press, 2013).

32 Ramsay Burt, *Ungoverning Dance: Contemporary European Theatre Dance and the Commons* (Oxford: Oxford University Press, 2017).

33 Van Assche, *Labor and Aesthetics in European Contemporary Dance: Dancing Precarity* (Cham: Palgrave Macmillan, 2020).

34 Bojana Kunst, *Artist at Work: Proximity of Art and Capitalism* (Hants: Zero Books, 2015).

35 Ibid., 1–3.

36 Marina Gržinić, Aneta Stojnić, and Miško Šuvaković (Eds.), *Regimes of Invisibility in Contemporary Art, Theory and Culture: Image, Racialization, History* (London: Palgrave Macmillan, 2017).

37 Marina Gržinić and Aneta Stojnić, *Shifting Corporealities in Contemporary Performance: Danger, Im/mobility and Politics* (Avant-Gardes in Performance) (London: Palgrave Macmillan, 2018).

38 Joe Kelleher, *Theatre & Politics* (Basingstoke: Palgrave Macmillan, 2009).

39 Nicholas Ridout, *Passionate Amateurs: Theatre, Communism, and Love* (Ann Arbor: The University of Michigan Press, 2013).

40 Alan Read, *The Dark Theatre: A Book About Loss* (London: Routledge, 2020).

41 Michael Shane Boyle, "Performance and Value: The Work of Theatre in Karl Marx's Critique of Political Economy," *Theatre Survey* 58, no. 1 (2017): 3–23.

42 See, for example, David Harvey's works *Marx, Capital and the Madness of Economic Reason* (Oxford: Oxford University Press, 2018); *Seventeen Contradictions and the End of Capitalism* (Oxford: Oxford University Press, 2014); *The Enigma of Capital and the Crises of Capitalism* (Oxford: Oxford University Press, 2010); *A Brief History of Neoliberalism* (Oxford: Oxford University Press, 2005).

43 Bourdieu, *Distinction*.

44 Éric Alliez and Maurizio Lazzarato, *Wars and Capital* (Semiotext(e), 2018). Last accessed March 3, 2019, from: https://mitpress.mit.edu/books/wars-and-capital.

45 Bidet, *Foucault with Marx*.

46 Stiegler, *For a New Critique of Political Economy*, 19.

47 Ibid., 25, emphasis in the original.

48 Ibid., 40.

49 Slavoj Žižek, *Living in the End Times* (London: Verso, 2010).

50 Katerina Paramana, *Performances of Thought, Resistance and Support: On the Potential of Performance in the Contemporary Moment* (PhD thesis, 2015).

51 Paramana, "The Animation of Contemporary Subjectivity in Tino Sehgal's *Ann Lee*."

52 Weeks, "Imagining Non-Work."

53 Berardi, "After the European Union."

54 Bernard Stiegler, *The Neganthropocene* (London: Open Humanities Press, 2018).

55 Stiegler, *For a New Critique of Political Economy*, 6, emphasis in the original.

56 Ibid.

57 Ashok Kumar, Adam Elliott-Cooper, Shruti Iyer, and Dalia Gebrial, "An Introduction to the Special Issue on Identity Politics," *Historical Materialism* 26, no. 2 (2018): 3–20. Kumar, Elliott-Cooper, Iyer, and Gebrial comment on the contrived ("socially constructed, yet naturalised") opposition between the terms "class politics" and "identity politics" (5):

> the Left's failure to articulate a compelling, rigorous history of identity-formation and, by extension, identity-oppression as

rooted in capitalist dynamics left a dangerous explanatory vacuum. Furthermore, it created an organisational culture of individualised, positionality politics that precluded the possibility of broad-based co-operation. . . . If *only* the personal can be political, then solidarity ceases to be desirable—let alone achievable. (ibid.)

Chi-Chi Shi and Annie Olaloku-Teriba suggest that we need to conceptualize identity-based politics outside a "liberal-capitalist logic" (ibid., 5–6), and Ashley Bohrer argues that what is necessary in order to "understand capitalist exploitation and oppression" but also "mobilise to overthrow it" is intersectional Marxism (ibid., 15). As Paul Gilroy puts it, "identity should be the basis for our politics, not our politics in-itself" (ibid., 14).

58 Cedric J. Robinson, *Black Marxism: The Making of the Black Radical Tradition* (Chapel Hill, NC: The University of North Carolina Press, 2000 [1983]).

Provocation 2

2 RECOGNIZING RACE AND CLASS IN DANCE
GONZALEZ RESPONSE TO PARAMANA

Anita Gonzalez

Not long ago I was leading a workshop for dance students about diversity, equity, and inclusion. We completed a cultural mapping exercise where students considered their geographic origins across generations, standing on different sections of an imaginary map to locate their cultural heritages. After thirty minutes of discussing geographic and racial differences, I asked if they would be willing to consider class origins by lining up according to their perceived class. An icy silence fell across the studio—downward eye focus, constricted breath. Some moved toward the perimeters of the studio space as if seeking refuge from an attack. Clearly, I had broached an unmentionable topic within the 2019 cultural landscape of the United States. This exercise was conducted at an elite public school where mostly upper-middle-class and wealthy students intermingled with a few middle- and working-class students. Why did they carry antipathy about discussing impacts of political economies on lived experiences?

Political economies affect all aspects of the dancer's life: training, aesthetics, employment, apparel, transit, and, ultimately, opportunity. Even aesthetic orientations of dance professionals ultimately depend on the economic realities of how individuals are able to enter into a world of professional dance practice. By this I mean choices about where to dance, which styles to engage in, reflect economic realities. A Bharatanatyam dancer, schooled in community spaces, understands aesthetics of hand gestures and complex rhythms in a way which may not resonate well with abstract nonrhythmic components of some postmodern dance. Consider what might be the trajectory of a street dancer who aspires to enter a world of concert dance. First prerequisites would be an ability to execute ballet combinations in a studio, usually with groups of women well versed in technical specificities of Euro-American dance. The student would need to understand French-based terminologies for leaps and turns, walks, and arm patterns. Without access to economic and social structures which support these knowledge epistemologies "inequality, precariousness and injustice prevail."[1] Only access to particular economies of wealth, culture, and social norms would enable this dancer's successful participation in the concert dance world.

Implicit in the lack of discussion about the impact of political economies on arts practices is a lack of discussion of inequality and the ethics of unequal distribution of opportunities for artists. Unequal access renders disempowered artists mute and invisible. How can we speak about diverse subjective positions if class cannot be discussed? What are the ethics of locating dance as unclassed labor within a society defined by gendered, classed, and racialized political economies? In an essay from the edited collection *British Dance, Black Routes*, Funmi Adewole states: "At times choreographers reject the subject position offered them by the commercial or artistic discourse of the time. They might feel they need to create a new subject position for themselves or their work if it is to be received in a way they consider appropriate."[2] Part of these subject positions involves acknowledgment of diverse economic circumstances. I believe intersectional identities are key to considerations of the impact of political economies. Black artists, even the wealthy ones, live in a political economy of disenfranchisement.

I am a middle-class Black academic and practitioner working in the Midwest of the United States, and my daily encounters with dancers underscore the impact of unconscious class bias on aspiring practitioners. How artists maintain their craft, arrive at the studio, or focus their artistry within a space where creativity can flourish, is influenced by cultural, social economic, and linguistic class paradigms. Like Bourdieu, I see dancers engaging in a sometimes-unacknowledged cultural capital when they enter the formal dance studio space. Dancers like to talk about concert performances, yet some dancers may not be able to engage in conversations about latest performances by new dance artists because they simply can't afford the ticket price. At the same time, academic writings and critical perspectives tend to privilege concert spaces or proscenium artistry where artists with access to certain performance aesthetics prevail. Yet the streets, the clubs, and other quotidian spaces nurture all kinds of dancing; dancing where different cultural codes are at work. The parkour dancer in the New York City subway needs to understand movements of crowds and moments of improvisation. Her economic reward comes when she is able to beguile a stranger, then captivate him with flips or turns. Her social class reveals itself through aesthetic styles and modes of engagement perhaps foreign to dancers working in formalized concert stages. Class affects each iterative, communicative moment.

Paul DiMaggio, in his essay "Sociological Perspective on the Face-to-Face Enactment of Class Distinction," acknowledges that North Americans embrace discussions of class reluctantly.[3] He suggests that conversations about class must move beyond Marxist definitions rooted in labor. He considers theories of Weber, Goffman, Bernstein, Bourdieu, Collin, and Erikson, before concluding: "People of every social class enter into encounters equipped with race, gender, and other characteristics that make it difficult to speak of pure class effects on interaction dynamics."[4] In the United States, it is difficult to discuss class without considering generational effects of race and gender on social constructions of access to wealth. I appreciate how DiMaggio ultimately considers scripted interactions as a means of negotiating class in cross-class encounters. This scripting and monitoring of class behavior across race and gender lines characterizes how dancers interact within the primarily nonverbal space of the studio.

There are other impacts of classed behavior to consider. Class hierarchies also depend upon patterns of social exclusion, distinctions of language use, coupled with perceptions of who is an outsider. Adrie Kusserow, for example, identifies different expressions of individualism across class lines in her essay "When Hard and Soft Clash: Class-Based Individualisms in Manhattan and Queens."[5] Approaching class through the lens of cultural anthropology, she uses field work to categorize preferred qualities of individualism across class lines. Middle-class respondents value softness and emotional responsiveness while working-class respondents believe toughness and discipline represent individualism. Differences like this manifest in how artists perceive their personal creative expression. Since some types of dance are construed as an individualistic interpretation of life expressed through physical agility, differing perspectives about what constitutes individualism impacts aesthetics. Within this context, "soft" and "hard" might result in differing attitudes about how best to enact empathies which might lead to social change. Social class inherently contributes to ways in which individuals navigate terrains of empathy.

Interventions in the macros of political economies begin in the micro. What is it like to arrive at the dance studio by public transportation instead of private car? How do you pay for training classes and at what cost to dietary or housing budgets? Does the dancer who learns on the street corner have the same access to a professional lifestyle as the dancer who receives daily training from a ballet master? Raced and gendered pathways intersect with access to ensure a consistent hierarchy among dance practitioners where political interventions are neutralized in part because those empowered to create disruptions are already representatives of an empowered economic class. Observations in the field lead me to believe that while political economies determine both aesthetics and life paths of dance practitioners, dance studios also offer possibilities for transcending class barriers.

Even though the field of dance exists within economic, classed structures, it has the capacity to trouble class categories through gestures of encounter. Like other forms of live performance, dance involves a collective engagement in breath. By breathing and moving together, dancers exchange in ways which can embody class, but can also break with social expectations. One person performs a balletic plié, another person squats, and together we negotiate subtleties of forms inherent in our differing expressive dynamics. Can we navigate class within corporeal exchanges? Collectives, formed by socially conscious individuals who dance together, have the potential to bring about changes which affect society. As political landscapes in the United States and the United Kingdom shift toward the right, is there a space for nuanced consideration of political economies in the dance studio as groundwork for understanding difference?

My entrance into political economies is necessarily influenced by experiences of race. Working in academia in the United States, I see great disparities in the way in which would-be dancers of differing skin colors gain access to the studio space. Those with resources arrive well equipped with an armor of classical ballet and contemporary modern dance training which allows them to navigate the complexities of an "across-the-floor" combination with linear and flowing components. Others, trained in techniques privileging torso movements or percussive phrases or isolated gestural moves, are less successful. The latter aesthetic, more common in African diasporic and Southeast Asian dances, comes from specific ethnic communities where dance emerges from traditions of storytelling through music and gesture. Even though cultural heritage may impact form, I want to untangle class from skin color. Many of our students of color come from wealthy, suburban backgrounds, but their colleagues may not know that. I wonder how bodies themselves resonate with presumptions about economic and social experiences. I'm interested in intersections and convergences across discussions of class and ethnicity.

Gender plays out differently in terms of class and access as well. A scarcity of men in dance programs coupled with ascriptions of fixed gender roles in many types of dancing makes economic access to commercial jobs unequal for men and women. Even though contemporary dance companies would like to work against stereotypical casting in concert dance, inequities of pay persist. Managers continue to welcome men into upper echelons of organizations, leaving women to manage laborious day-today operations of studios.

Our book project asks its contributors to observe how economic disparities influence dancers and dance makers. I am struck by two differing descriptions of walking which reference economic class. Katerina Paramana begins her dissertation project about "the role of art and the artist in relation to society" with a description of watching neighborhood passersby on Deptford High Street in London in December 2014.[6] She notices gentrification, rent gaps, and other economic markers, articulating different economies she sees embedded in her relationship to the world which surrounds her. In a similar way, Anna Scott, in her essay from *Black Performance Theory* titled "Cityscapes Ethnospheres,"[7] walks the streets considering the implications of her physical and social presence in space. In ten sections, she reflects on the meaning of her walk. Steps meander, retrace, reconstruct social consciousness, and revisit spatial awareness. She ends her essay about spatial encounters on a disturbing note which speaks to economic disparities in a historical way. She describes the "Dancing Darkey Boy," a nineteenth-century entertainer who flat foots on the docks in New York City dancing for eels to pay for his meals. Scott writes: "He keeps going. Does he slip on the coins? They throw things at him. Is he now extracted from his labor? Is he surplus? Or his feet? Is it in his smile? The extraction point? Maneuvering, manipulating, he keeps dancing."

Her point is that for this historical "Dancing Darkey Boy," an anonymous popular entertainer, his performance is perceived and constrained by imaginations about his race. His membership in the lower echelons of the economy is just one part of the social ramifications of his dance performance. He dances for coins while disregarding the insults of those who view his performance through a racialized lens. The economy of the performance is in clear view. The observers throw coins at him as he dances and smiles. This child has no access to sanctioned performance spaces where critics will write about his work. Instead we know of him by grainy images documenting the poverty and marvels of the nineteenth-century docks.

In some ways, this racial and economic construct continues to contain those who enter economies of dance at the intersection of race, class, and gender. What space is there for social activism when one is busking for a living, using the corporeality of the dancing body to earn wages needed to eat for a day? The dancing boy smiles and acknowledges his class. He is working for the money. If there is notoriety attached to this economic exchange he may not care. The activism is in tricking the crowd to pass the hat. This short book focuses on the relation of performance and dance, broadly conceived, to contemporary political economies. Even before a performer arrives at the classroom door, multiple legacies of race, class, and gender are at play as moving bodies navigate a sometimes-treacherous space of artistry and activism.

We will be asking a cohort of scholars and artists to theorize about impact, meanings, and relations between bodies and political economies. One component of the process will be for the contributors to bring expertise from differing disciplinary backgrounds to the project. As editors, we are interested in what writers see, and how they respond to multiple economies at work.

Notes

1 Katerina Paramana, "Performance, Dance and Political Economy: A Provocation," this volume.

2 Funmi Adewole, "The Construction of the Black Dance/African People's Dance Sector in Britain: Issues Arising for the Conceptualization of Related Dance and Choreographic Practices," in Christy Adair and Ramsay Burt (eds.), *British Dance: Black Routes* (London: Routledge, 2017), 125–48.

3 Paul DiMaggio, "Sociological Perspectives on Face-to-Face Enactment of Class Distinction," in Susan Fiske and Hazel Marcus (eds.), *Facing Social Class: How Societal Rank Influences Interaction* (New York: Russel Sage Foundation, 2012), 15–38.

4 Ibid., 29.

5 Adrie Kusserow, "When Hard and Soft Clash: Class-Based Individualisms in Manhattan and Queens," in Susan Fiske and Hazel Marcus (eds.), *Facing Social Class: How Societal Rank Influences Interaction* (New York: Russel Sage Foundation, 2012), 176–94.

6 Katerina Paramana, "Introduction," *Performances of Thought, Resistance and Support: On the Potential of Performance in the Contemporary Moment* (PhD thesis, 2015).

7 Anna B. Scott, *Black Performance Theory*, ed. Thomas F. DeFrantz and Anita Gonzalez (Durham: Duke University Press, 2014), 158–67.

DIALOGUE 1
CONTROL OF BODIES

Nina Power, in her chapter, "A World beyond the Captured Body," unpicks the ways in which the state measures and captures bodies, and what happens when they escape measurement and capture, even temporarily. Marc Arthur's chapter, "Choreographing Rage," examines Regina José Galindo's performance *Tierra* and ACT UP's action *Seize the FDA* by AIDS activists at the Federal Drug Administration's (FDA) headquarters. Both chapters in Dialogue 1 describe the relationship between bodies and political economy as one of control and consider ways in which bodies-performance-dance might subvert this relationship.

3 A WORLD BEYOND THE CAPTURED BODY
Nina Power

(A Response to Videos from the Playlist[1])

In this chapter, I discuss a performance involving a self-selecting portion of the public that took place at Tate Live's Performance Room and a documentary in the form of a college class delivered by an artist. I am interested in what these two cultural productions can tell us about the ways in which bodies are distributed in space: what happens when different bodies are measured and captured by the state, and what happens when they are (temporarily at least) not measured or captured?

Spatial Confessions

Cvejić and de Smedt's *Spatial Confessions* is a highly choreographed, deadpan piece of public theatrical direction, highlighting above all else the way in which the current system of neoliberal capitalism seeks to measure and capture our singularities and differences, thus rendering us indistinguishable from one another. In the performance, a voice commands the volunteers to "take positions" in a literal, physical, embodied way (rather than, let us say, the usual way we might understand "position-taking" as an act of asserting one's opinion in speech or in writing). This is done on the basis of often-bizarre types of differentiation—for example, who has more money between the participants (though how strange this particular distinction is beyond the room of the performance is seriously open to question, given how much money matters in the current system) or who thinks that sex is "overrated." Participants are, for example, asked to stand on the left or right side of the room, depending on their responses to the question, or to put themselves in a rough order depending on what they think the other people in the room have or represent.

By pushing opinions, feelings, identities, representations, and positions to an absurd point, by making bodies move to physical positions that "reflect" political or personal positions, *Spatial Confessions* blows apart the poll-like, measure, regime of quantity that we all live under. Why are we being measured all the time? Who cares about our opinions? Do we? Does anybody beyond marketers and the algorithm? Are our opinions who we are or are we more than that? Some of the bodies in Cvejić and de Smedt's piece hover midway between left and right, usually the only options available to the participants. What does it mean to be somewhere in the middle of an opinion, to be unsure, to be ambivalent? Are we allowed to be ambivalent on matters of the day? Increasingly it seems impossible *not* to have an opinion, not to take a stance, not to have a line. Is it possible to opt out of a position, physically or politically or socially? Can one be indifferent to the issues of the day, let's say, such as Brexit, the refugee crisis, the question of sex/gender, or even politics as a whole?

What to make, also, of the "confessional" aspect of Cvejić and de Smedt's work? Here bodies are moved by the decisions made by their owners, although perhaps the bodies move first and the decision comes later, by a split-second. The "authoritarian" nature of the authors' questions represents a certain kind of "control," but the decision is handed over to the participants—they take on the orders willingly.

So what does it mean to "confess" with one's body? We tend to think of confessions as verbal or literary efforts, religious, psychoanalytic, or social works. What can the body, or bodies, tell us about confession? The body may "keep the score" as one way of thinking about trauma and our bodies often do "betray" us by blushing, recoiling, flinching, laughing, or becoming aroused, among other things. But to use one's whole body as an instrument of confession indicates another kind of discourse: if one is captured by guilt or acts that one must expiate in confession, what can the collective confessional body tell us about what burdens we all carry with us? There is in the end a kind of collective psychoanalytic dimension too to Cvejić and de Smedt's piece, where we come to understand that the things that make us who we are, are perhaps not what we think they might be in the first place: who we are together is stronger and more interesting. The political economy that makes us "individuals" of necessity overlooks the possibility and the joy of being a "social individual," that is to say, an individual whose meaning only comes to light in the wake of group existence.

Everybody in the Place

Group existence or collective being is very much at the heart of Jeremy Deller's piece as well. The rave period—the so-called second summer of love that began roughly in 1988–9 in the UK and which Deller presents in *Everybody in the Place* as a kind of pedagogical lecture to contemporary college-age students—appears as a kind of fantastical mirage of the past, a time when people moved their bodies in strange contortions and broke out of certain types of identity. Rave, at its best, was a reclamation of the land and an understanding that it belonged to every*body*; that is to say, that the illegal temporary occupation of enclosed and private land was an experiential reminder of the possibility of different social relations, of different political arrangements. It was a party to which everybody was invited.

By presenting his history of rave in the context of political economy—the policing of the miners' strike, the inequality of Thatcherism, police violence, the punishment of those who wanted to enjoy Stonehenge, and other historic and spiritual sites in the UK—Deller situates what might at first appear as simple acts of collective hedonism as serious breakthroughs in the mind-expansion of the participants in rave culture. Here was a movement, he indicates, that, by virtue of transgressing the bounds of what the state permitted, drew attention to deep questions regarding the ownership of land in the UK. What would it mean if the land did in fact belong to everyone? Why does private property exist? Can we live in a kind of permanent celebration of the existence of all of our bodies? In the ecstatic moment? There is no doubt that rave was a permanently transformative experience for many who were there and carry the experience with them many years later.

By making rave into a teaching experience for the students in the film, and, in turn, by making the viewer the audience for this lesson, Deller creates an interesting double pedagogical moment: we are being taught by the teacher who is teaching others. The lesson is multiple: the instructions of history should not pass us by, but also, what might it mean to remember rave today? Is a third summer of love possible in an era of mobile phones, the internet, and many other advanced forms of alienated technology? What might it mean today to "take to the land," to feel a sense of belonging to the countryside, particularly to those who live in the cities? To move bodies collectively in trance-like states for hours in nature?

Beyond the Captured Body

Both productions point in different ways to a world beyond the *captured body*, what we could call the "body of the state," that is to say, the body as it can and is kept in its place. I would like to suggest in this short text that dance and movement in these two productions—dance and movement that is, in each case, amateur, popular, free, voluntary—point toward expressions of freedom that relate to place, that is to say, to the land and to the distribution of bodies on and in the land, and across different systems, in different but interestingly compatible ways.

We are alerted to what could be called "the positional" in the respective titles of the pieces: Deller's "place" and Cvejić and de Smedt's "spatial." The "place" of Deller's work comes from a rave track, and could refer to, among other things, the place of the nightclub, which does indeed feature in his documentary. But it can also refer to larger places, such as the land as such, namely the countryside where many of the illegal raves took place during the end of the 1980s and beginning of the 1990s. Cvejić and de Smedt's "spatial" is more ambiguous in some ways, referring to, among other things, the space of the gallery in which the work takes place, but also the "space" of distribution itself, which is to say, the way in which our bodies and identities, not to mention our thoughts, feelings, opinions, and other things that may or may not be "measurable," are recorded in space. And this space can be the space of online (the churn of social media opinions, for example, harvested by algorithms and fed back to the machine in a kind of permanent, insomniac feast), the space of work (our role in the economy, our status as workers, the kinds of jobs we might do), the space beyond work (if there is any such space), the space of "character," of "personality," of interests and desires. We are always located in space "somewhere." Our phones locate us, we have a geoposition mapped by satellites. But we are also in space in multiple other ways—in the cosmos, in nature, in company, in our thoughts, and so on.

Both pieces seek, through humor and order in the case of *Spatial Confessions* and through pedagogy and history in the case of *Everybody in the Place*, to present the possibility of a world unbound by measurement. The first piece seeks to do so by exploding the desire to measure by taking it to an extreme; the second by invoking a recent past, where many bodies took up the cause of enjoyment and dancing against the state, causing it to panic and introduce new legislation regarding the use of land and edicts against travelling, and to ban, to great bemusement as well as horror, "repetitive beats" (see 1994's Criminal Justice and Public Order Act). What do these two explorations tell us about the relationship between dance (or movement) and political economy? In the first place, they evidence how movement can easily trouble the state and the state's way of measuring and capturing bodies; in the second, they present alternatives to the "normal order of things." In my reading of the work, Cvejić and de Smedt do this by drawing very detailed attention to the bureaucratic pathologies of a measured life, and, by making these pathologies into a kind of game, they attempt to diminish their power over us. In contrast, Deller opens us a new possibility of relating to different kinds of collectivity by compiling documentary footage of a moment of the recent past in which people moved as if the land and space belonged to them (and thus to everybody) and presenting it to students today. While both works deal with the state and only indirectly with political economy, the latter element is never far away. Cvejić and de Smedt draw attention to the ways in which people are divided by class and income, among other things, and Deller makes clear how rave threatened the idea of private property as well as broke the bounds of the kinds of enjoyment (alcohol culture, primarily) permitted by the state. The uncaptured body in both cases is a collective, joyful body, a body that together recognizes difference and explodes it in merry laughter, in topsy-turvyness, in rebellion, in abandon.

Both works ultimately are on the side of the hopeful for a world beyond the captured body. Could we break once and for all with state measurement and capture of all kinds? What would it mean to be free, truly free, to be outside, to make and take our own measure of space and place? Both pieces invoke humor and present the desirability of bodies becoming collective bodies without eliminating difference. Rave culture was also about the recognition of difference, how different we all are, but also how cool these differences are. If only there is enough time and space to express and embrace these differences, we need never go back to state time and state place. We could stay outside forever and we would make our own rules. And life would become art, and all our gestures would be a kind of dance.

Note

1 Bojana Cvejić and Christine de Smedt, *Spatial Confessions*, 2014. Available at: https://www.youtube.com/watch?v=_PEDcLVVUdc; Jeremy Deller, *Everybody in the Place: An Incomplete History of Britain 1984-1992*, 2018. https://vimeo.com/278494935.

4 CHOREOGRAPHING RAGE
Marc Arthur

(A Response to Videos from the Playlist[1])

Rage endures past oppression and exceeds anger. It is a drive that is blind with audacity and that confronts the moral and ethical conditions that produce human suffering. Rage is at once mythic and bitterly real. Its pernicious qualities must be embodied and made present to foment intervention. Rage must be shared to support an economy of optimism. From its eruptions in the immediacy of subjective experience, rage can be sustained as a collective force that fuels resistance and change.

I was born in the early 1980s and grew up in Arizona where AIDS always felt distant and removed from my suburban daily life. If there was rage produced by the AIDS crisis when I was a child, it appeared in snippets or in overly dramatized scenes. It was something to fear. When I came out in high school, it quickly became clear that with my sexuality I was inheriting an entire culture of AIDS-related queer dispossession, stigmatization, and rage. I do not like the word "inheritance" though. It is too genealogical, too clean in its delineation between a past and present. It verges on the nostalgic, which forecloses narratives of AIDS that are ongoing and that are complicated by intersecting histories of negligence.

"ACT UP & ACT NOW Seize Control of the FDA," October 11, 1988 (5:15–11 Minutes)

The impulse to inherit or feel nostalgic about AIDS does not capture the hot and angry feelings that pass through my body while I watched the video of ACT UP's "Seize the FDA" action at the Federal Drug Administration's (FDA) headquarters in Rockville, Maryland (1988) (see Figure 1). The video is a potent chronical of rage that captures a flash point in the battle between AIDS activists and the FDA. The FDA at the time refused to make life-saving drugs accessible when HIV was spreading at unprecedented rates in the late 1980s because they needed to undergo clinical trials. As protestors shout "one death every thirty minutes," their urgency is deployed explicitly as rage at the FDA's refusal to speed up the drug approval process for acquiring experimental drugs—their only hope at the time for survival. The thousands of protestors were also demanding agency and a voice in the development of experimental drugs through their own embodied knowledge. The unity of actions and organizing was an effort to remake the healthcare economy.

FIGURE 1 ACT UP "Seize Control of the FDA" action at the Food and Drug Administration headquarters in Rockville, Maryland, on October 11, 1988. Photo by T. L. Litt.

A tension between history and the present emerges for me while watching the video. As a queer person, I feel connected to the unity of the protestors' rage, to their indignation against the government's role in exacerbating the death toll of AIDS-related deaths, and the FDA's negligence during this period. It is like watching a dance to which you already know the choreography. And yet, I am equally aware that the fight for equal access to healthcare is far from over and that today, HIV disproportionately impacts People of Color, people in poverty, and young people.

I first saw this video in my early twenties. I was working as a dramaturge for Jack Waters and Peter Cramer, two queer HIV-positive artists and activists in New York City. Jack was taking his antiretroviral drugs and telling me about the hallucinatory waking dreams they gave him. He mentioned the protest at the FDA headquarters as a pivotal turning point in the biomedical trajectory of HIV biopharmaceutical management. In the video, activists wear lab coats or white sweatshirts that read "Person with AIDS" in red paint, highlighting the cultural narratives of contamination that were coalescing around their bodies as a political identity. In one poignant moment, a few police officers attempt to move a cluster of protestors who are linked arm in arm. As the police struggle to manage them, rage is condensed not only through their gaze but also in their physical refusal to move or disconnect from one another. I can see rage reacts across and between them, and I picture a topographic map of that force circulating within my own body. This circulation of rage is a kind of economy of optimism that gestures toward the future while looking to physical practices of resistance in the past.

As I watch the crowd of hundreds cheer when an activist attaches a "Silence = Death" banner to the front of the FDA headquarters façade, I see their actions through the lens of dance. Susan Leigh Foster has thought of choreography as a means to unpack how bodies alter structures of power. She asks of ACT UP protests like this one: "how have these bodies been trained, and how has that training mastered, cultivated, or facilitated their impulses?; what do they share that allows them to move with one another?; what kind of relationship do they establish with those who are watching their actions?"[2] Her provocations bring light to how knowledge is created and shared between bodies, and help me to understand the politicized way dancers put pressure on the economies which seek to profit from their bodies. This is apparent in the way that protestors move together in unison, the efforts they make to refuse to break apart from holding one another, that they are altering and resisting how they have been trained to move in public. They have developed their own choreographic language for survival.

Jack and Peter, the aforementioned artists, also create languages of survival and resistance. Both professionally trained dancers, they met dancing with the Battery Dance Company in the early 1980s. Their creative, activist, and personal lives have always intertwined to create a messy and uniquely queer theater that rarely follows a logic that is easily digested. They were involved in many ACT UP demos and actions and have extended their commitment to AIDS advocacy through their many organizing and artistic endeavors.

I have always wondered how AIDS activism changed their dance technique. While in Hamburg for a residency, we went dancing together at a gay nightclub one evening. It was difficult not to notice their formal training. Yet their posture and intentionality somehow willed open a zone of anarchic motion, making an otherwise casual dance floor more rigorously disordered. I noticed not only how my own form changed but also others' at the club. I felt encouraged to develop a movement vocabulary that undermines distinctions between technique and freedom.

Regina José Galindo, *Tierra*, 2013 (2:26–9:09 Minutes)

The Guatemalan artist Regina José Galindo's *Tierra* (2013) is not about AIDS, but it palpably shares the quality of rage that can be witnessed in AIDS activism of the 1980s. While later in the piece Galindo stands naked as a bulldozer digs into the earth all around her, at this point of the video that I am writing about here, I watch her dig her hands and arms into the ground near a tree as a small audience watches in the background. It is an austere scene that reminds me of Cuban American artist Ana Mendieta's earth body imprint pieces. At first, I am struck by how Galindo channels those who were murdered, taking on the weight of their lives with her body. Galindo is also responding to state-sponsored political violence. Her performance confronts Guatemalan dictator Efraín Ríos Montt's genocidal war crimes, which fully came to light in 2013 with charges for crimes against humanity. During the country's bloody civil war, following his coup in 1982, the dictator systemically had hundreds of thousands of innocent civilians murdered.

One of the most obvious ways that this piece evokes a shared sense of rage with the "Seize the FDA" video is that they are both tied to President Ronald Regan's economic and political US policies. The Reagan administration's failure to respond to AIDS is perhaps best evidenced by the infamous words of Gary Bauer, the chairman of Reagan's Special Working Group on the Family: "I suspect that he was told, 'AIDS is something you don't have to worry about, Mr. President, because, after all, it affects homosexuals, it affects drug abusers, it affects sexually promiscuous people, Mr. President. And these are not your people.'"[3] When, in 1987, after 25,644 lives had already been lost from AIDS-related illnesses, Reagan finally uttered the word "AIDS" for the first time, he announced that his administration would look stymying infection rates through moral rather than medical interventions.[4] Such a viewpoint, that homosexuality and drug use was to blame for the spread of HIV, was supported and implemented by the Regan administration's economic policies of underfunding AIDS research at the FDA. During this same decade, there was no lack of funding for helicopters and guns for Ríos Montt's *coup d'état*. In 1982, Regan visited Ríos Montt in Guatemala City declaring "President Ríos Montt is a man of great personal integrity and commitment. . . . I know he wants to improve the quality of life for all Guatemalans and to promote social justice."[5] Despite evidence of growing human rights violations, particularly against Indigenous populations, Reagan's administration sent $4 million in aid for military supplies, bypassing congress in the process. In 1983 a CIA memo described increasing number of bodies "appearing in ditches and gullies."[6]

This is where Galindo's *Tierra* is staged: at a site in Guatemala where the state military would bring enemies and kill them, push their bodies into a ditch, and cover them with dirt using a hydraulic bulldozer. Galindo's tactic of politicizing a space through performance in this manner echoes AIDS activists who would use their bodies to protest Regan's violent negligence. Galindo holds the government accountable for their economically underwritten state violence with her still and unmoving body, which in the context of this site's history, is deeply charged with rage.

Sharing Rage

Rage is something that resonates through Galindo and the AIDS activists at an axis of interrelations between history, subjectivity, and political resistance. Opened up by their movement, they create environments of feeling that evoke dance theorist Mark Franko's prioritization of the body as a site of affect transmission. Franko believes that the dancers are inherently attuned to and affected by social forces: "[s]ince bodies are at the root of lived experience, it can be shown that dance works with the same materials from which the organizing social force of ideology must be drawn."[7] Built on the social force and ideology of rage, these two videos exhibit movement that can critique the politicization of economies. Galindo and the AIDS activists use their bodies to redefine how bodies are violently arranged within economic agendas and ideologies of control. Furthermore, they offer clues for how to activate rage in bodies which have been treated as inventory or valueless.

In Franko's prioritization of dance as a site of affect transmission, he distinguishes affects from emotions, noting that "affect occurs when dance has transmitted the essence of a feeling; emotion occurs when dance has transmitted a specific and temporally contingent feeling."[8] While watching these videos, emotions are certainly present in my experience, but rage hits me differently. It permits a kinetic political friction, characterized by an affect that cannot account for the choreographic excess of bodies that circulate and spawn unconscious drives of fury in others. Rage, constructed as a total exertion on boundaries and restrictions, and invoked as it is in these two videos, retains a haptic memory of movement against violent forces. When it arrives on my computer screen it has already dissolved, exceeded, or mutated in some way. I am interested in the transmissibility of the affect of political passions, especially those experiences of rage that circulate through me but which I did not experience or witness. As it changes and shifts between forms and generations, rage continues to be productive. Dance can be a method of sharing rage that allows artists to break the fantasy that economics are not embodied, and to demand a role in political decision-making as it comes to shape social and cultural worlds.

Notes

1 "ACT UP & ACT NOW Seize Control of the FDA," October 11, 1988: https://www.youtube.com/watch?v=s70aCOflRgY&t=817s and Regina José Galindo's, *Tierra: https://youtu.be/RdCdZnVB6bw*.

2 Susan Leigh Foster, "Choreographies of Protest," *Theatre Journal* 55 (2003): 397.

3 Gerald Strober and Deborah Hart Strober, *Reagan: The Man and His Presidency* (Houghton Mifflin, 1998), 136.

4 Ibid., 138.

5 Jennifer Schirmer, *The Guatemalan Military Project: A Violence Called Democracy* (Philadelphia: University of Pennsylvania Press, 1998), 33.

6 National Security Archive, Washington, D.C. February 1983 (Ríos Montt Gives Carte Blanche to Archivos to Deal with Insurgency) CIA, secret cable.
7 Mark Franko, *The Work of Dance: Labor, Movement, and Identity in the 1930s* (Middletown, CT: Wesleyan, 2002), 59.
8 Ibid., 9.

DIALOGUE 2
COMMODIFICATION OF BODIES

In "Honesty and the Body," Nina Power suggests that our gestures and movements are not our own for our bodies constantly serve two nonhuman masters: the market (and the "alien rhythms of capital" to which we move) and the "imagined group that judges us" (on the internet and social media). Alexandrina Hemsley, in her performative chapter "Feeling My Way Through Several Beginnings," offers a picture of the complex and intertwined challenges of working as a dance artist. She suggests that in capitalism powerlessness is capitalized and the powerful are protected. In Dialogue 2, both chapters critique the manner in which bodies, gestures, emotions, and feelings are commodified in neoliberal capitalism and dominated by its mechanics. They propose a reconnection to our body that demonstrates care for self and others. Dance is presented as a potential way out.

5 HONESTY AND THE BODY
Nina Power

(A Response to the Editors' Provocations)

Our gestures betray us, but not in the way we might have once thought in the sense that the way we move reveals some deeper truth about what we think or feel. Rather today our gestures betray us in that they further separate us from who or what we are, because our movements are not our own; they are other-directed. The other, in this instance, is not necessarily a person, but a combination of the market and the big other. In other words, our bodies serve two masters, neither of which is fully human. We move to the alien rhythm of capital and we present our bodies to the vision not of God but of the imagined group that judges us.

God now resides if at all in the visual, not the omniscient, omnibenevolent all-mighty, nor even the surveillance of communist or capitalist police-states, but rather the surveillance that we appear to have freely chosen, which is to say the self-surveillance that we take upon ourselves, daily, or nearabouts, in order to send images and messages to the world. This is not done in the name of the good, or in the name of a spiritual being, or in relation to a calculus of good deeds, but rather on this earth, here, now, and for the little other pretending to be the big other. There are many more images than we can process, even many more images of ourselves than we can ever look at, let alone expect anyone else to.

We move in the world at the dictates also not exactly of our choosing. The market, the *oikos* made monstrous, made dominant, has replaced the space of politics and of anything else—including justice, love, poetry, the good, or anything else we might imagine—with its own demands, which we in turn anthropomorphize and internalize: the market is depressed, we are sad. We must work in order to survive, thus we must in ways that will generate money to keep us alive. This includes—how could it not?—the way we move our body, what we do with it, our gestures, the way we hold ourselves. Our body is a workplace. We could call this a choreography of the zero. The invention of zero is also the code of the market and the internalization of number; thus we move our body to abstractions that, in turn, are incarnated. We must get a job, we must be workers, we must be good workers, we are always on display at work and in play. We are binary code. In this way we are "not ourselves," because we are performing all the time for two, intertwined deities, the market and the other, the market-other. We cannot be honest because we do not express what we feel. We cannot express what we feel because we can no longer feel what it is that we feel, because our feelings have been simultaneously externalized and commodified, and we ourselves do this all the time without thinking and without remembering that we are still alive.

So, we are caught between these static images, and sometimes videos, of our movements that perhaps look like expressions of our inner being, but whose relation might be disjointed. This is of course not to say that the way we move must be "authentic" or that there is no room for masks, play, the inhabiting of other poses, performing, and so on. These are all modes of being that tie us to deep traditions of human meaning and symbolism. But today we are also up against a kind of uncanny valley of movement. We are in extreme proximity to things that move a little like us, but are not "natural" as such. We might argue that all human invention is natural because *we* are natural and therefore even the most artificial of our products have a kind of reality and determinism, but we are now always undoubtedly competing with the robot, the doll, the puppet, with the creatures we have created.

We are thus uncanny to ourselves. Our animal nature is subsumed under a weight of unreality, modernity, civilization. We live in the pharmacopornographic era, as Preciado would have it, where our libido is channeled directly through drugs of all kinds and our vision and fantasy life is dominated by images of desire flowing back toward us.[1] We are not exactly passive in the face of all this, but rather bewildered, stultified.

And what of the body in all this? Have we made of it a new religion, a material cult? Icons, in the form of images of bodies to worship, are everywhere, these static representations of who we are, who we should be, or should not be. But what is the relationship between bodies, capitalism, and religion? Is capitalism a cult of bodies? Undoubtedly, yes.

In a short fragment entitled "Capitalism and Religion," Walter Benjamin suggests that "capitalism is a pure religious cult, perhaps the most extreme there ever was."[2] The reason why capitalism is such a successful, all-encompassing cult that "knows no special dogma, no theology," as Benjamin puts it, is because of its permanent duration: "Capitalism is the celebration of the cult *sans rêve et sans merci*."[3] Without dream and without mercy. Capitalism needs no "rules," as it were, no commandments to follow, moral code, ritual directions, because it is impossible to imagine anything outside of the ongoing rites we find ourselves in.

It is understood that capitalism steals our time, transmutes finite existence into profit, but what Benjamin asks us to imagine is that instead of an unbalanced dialectic of work and play in which work dominates and we dream of work even in the weekends when we are "free," we are instead trapped in something much more nightmarish: a perpetual celebration of the cult that we have forgotten is a festival. Thus, if we were to follow Benjamin's train of thought, we are trapped in celebration, an orgy of excess of destruction ("play") that we have been tricked into understanding as its total opposite ("work," which is to say, coerced labor). We can see this in the ways in which sacred substances, ritual libations, right down to every last thing—meat, alcohol, drugs, theater, violence, sex, music, friendship—have been incorporated into the everyday, into "work," they *are* "work." You can spend your money, if you have some, on whatever you like ("you earned it!"). No one can stop you celebrating Dionysus on your own every evening, because there is no ritual context and no community to organize such a thing. Thus, everything sacred is made mundane and horizontal, and eternally destructive because it has no meaning, and it happens all the time, and this is what it means to be "free." Is there pleasure arising from play? Perhaps: but on set terms.

As Benjamin puts it: "Here there is no 'weekday,' no day that would not be a holiday in the awful sense of exhibiting all sacred pomp—the extreme exertion of worship."[4] It is of course exhausting to be attending a festival all the time: imagine the most wrecked you've ever felt at the highest (or lowest) point of the night and being stuck in that state forever, as you attempt all the other things you "must" do in your life. Capitalist modernity, as Marx noted, smashed and dissolved religious ecstasies in the logic of exchange, it drowned all higher feeling in a logic of sameness, all place in a kind of generalized non-place.[5] Thus we are everywhere and no one, and how we are captured reminds us not so much about the specificity of where we happen to be but rather the generality of being as such. And it is an embodied being that belongs to no one, a pure flatness, the shopping mall as model for distracted consumerist existence. The body as shopping bag.

There is today no experience outside of its capturability, outside of its memorability. Nothing can be forgotten. The high points of a group ecstatic experience are splintered and fragmented into tiny pieces, for which everyone remains conscious throughout, because all time is the same, and everything is recorded. What we have, perhaps, is a kind of hyperenchantment of the world rather than a disenchantment, where everything is "magical" but in an obscure, fallen, and menacing way. We are surrounded by forces we do not control, but that swirl around us, that terrify us. We do not know how our own bodies fit into this frame, or what power they themselves possess.

If we start from this idea of modernity not as disenchantment but as hyperenchantment, where festival has been generalized but forgotten, we can ask how it is to be a moving body in this matrix, how we feel, if we can feel at all. We are not in a post-magical age, or a post-religious age, but rather these things are everywhere but buried. All the mechanisms that magic and religion identified and had a solution for—fate, sin, guilt, uncertainty, the inexplicable, human violence, and resentment—still exist. We are not beyond them just because we pretend to be "civilized" or "modern" or "cynical." We are filled with the same emotions as our ancestors.

How does capitalism attempt to quell the disquiet that persists, despite the great reduction of everything to exchange? For Benjamin, "capitalism essentially serves to satisfy the same worries, anguish, and disquiet formerly answered by so-called religion."[6] In this sense, it is not that religion "feeds into" capitalism, as Weber identified, but rather that capitalism directly takes over its functions. Yet it cannot effectively, nor does it want to, serve every function that ritual and rites provided. Benjamin suggests that capitalism might be:

> the first case of a blaming, rather than a repenting cult .... An enormous feeling of guilt not itself knowing how to repent, grasps at the cult, not in order to repent for this guilt, but to make it universal, to hammer it into consciousness and finally and above all to include God himself in this guilt, in order to finally interest him in repentance.[7]

Guilt is another name for debt. It resides not only in our consciousness, as Benjamin has it, but in our bodies too. Thus we live in a gigantic matrix of debt: we are guilty for being born, for existing, for continuing to exist, in our relations to others. We are not allowed to expiate any of this within the current system, and there is no hierarchy that we could appeal to, at least according to the terms of the system itself. So we oscillate back and forth, uncertain what freedom could possibly mean, and carrying an inexplicably great burden around with us, because we don't know exactly how things work, its logic is hidden from view, as is the full expression of our capacities and our ability to be. We feel guilty for the other, people we have never met, the environment, for ourselves. Is guilt a useful mood for politics? Can we flourish here? How does guilt manifest itself in our bodies? Can we ever expiate this burden?

"There has to be more to life than killing yourself to survive" sings Richard Dawson on "Fulfilment Centre."[8] This "more to life"—where can we say it resides, if it does at all? What do we have with us? Our body is sometimes a mystery to us, yet it is all we have. When our gestures are not careful, that is to say, when we do not take care of ourselves, or the world, or of each other, we are signaling our distress with the existing state of affairs.

It is always possible to become careless, through misery, through nihilism, through despair: when our guilt outweighs our ability to bear it. When our bodies rebel against being puppets, when we no longer want to make our body and mind a machine for the market or pose for the big other.

What then of the allure of honesty? The honest body? Can we make our body honest in resistance against these mechanics of domination? Can we reconnect our body to what we feel and express these feelings in a way that also exhibits care? Is "dance" one of the names for this reconnection? Cynicism has all-too-often made us accept the disconnect between our bodies and our feelings, as if they were not the same things. It is possible to pretend not to feel, to turn masks inwards, to place the sad face mask in a place where no one else can see it, to feel its empty eyes and mouth pushed up against our skin from the inside. And meanwhile, the happy mask is on our face, in service, playing the role of external mediator.

But our eyes do not glow, they cannot gain energy from the eyes of others, we look down, we are ashamed of our own inconsistency. Where and when can we be ourselves, when we sell our souls every day to survive in this never-ending misery-go-round? Perhaps in collective dance—like a rave, or other loosely and perhaps illegal and unprompted gatherings of people moving—we approach something like a spontaneous game-playing, even within the constraints described here. Game-playing, that is to say, a qualitative and non-calculative dynamic, whose rules are deduced from its own character, a kind of collective joy that transcends both the labor of work and the enforced jollity of the festival without the let-up discussed earlier. "Dance" understood in its most general sense might have a privileged relation to this kind of rule-breaking. As Katerina Paramana puts it:

> Dance is very skilled at "seeing" time and space and the relationship of the body to them, at finding ways to negotiate, organise, create and break rules, find joy in being in the same space and time with others, working

with others, understanding the body—its mechanics, flow, experience and relation to other bodies—and listening to [it], its rhythms and needs.⁹

And what does being "honest," in spontaneous movement, the kind of honesty I am trying to defend here, really mean? When we use the word "honest" we might have in mind someone we can trust, someone who tells you the truth, or at least will be fair in their dealings with you. You can be poor and honest—perhaps it is easier to be, in fact.

But earlier meanings of the word were weighted a little differently. In the early fourteenth century, "honesty" meant something closer to "honor" and involved behaving in a just and virtuous way to oneself as well as to others.¹⁰ What has become of these lofty ideals? They have become destroyed, a kind of joke, something corrupted by the hypocritical way, they have been wielded by those intent on doing the opposite. We have no need of "honor" today, indeed it might be something of a hindrance, because it would entail that people did not do things they believed were wrong. And who today can afford to have principles? Who today can be honorable? Whose body gets to be honest?

Perhaps being "honest" is more simple than we might think. We have perhaps come to believe that what is complicated is "good," that we should fill our lives with objects and we become distracted by every little thing, every little thread that goes nowhere. Our body is torn to pieces like Pentheus by the Maenads at the festival, the one we have forgotten we have been forced to attend. Perhaps this is a more honest way to die, torn apart, and sacrificed by those in a frenzy who mistake you for a wild pig. Perhaps this is the state we find ourselves in in any case, torn limb from limb and then eaten alive. No wonder we strive for integrity in pictures, to present an image of the whole, when there is no unity to be found today in our bodies, ourselves, or anywhere else.

Notes

1 See Preciado's *Testo-Junkie: Sex, Drugs, and Biopolitics in the Pharmacopornographic Era*, trans. Bruce Benderson (New York City: The Feminist Press, 2013).

2 Walter Benjamin, "Capitalism and Religion," in Eduardo Mendieta (ed.), *The Frankfurt School on Religion: Key Writings by the Major Thinkers* (New York and London: Routledge, 2004), 259–62, p. 259.

3 Ibid., 259.
4 Ibid.
5 Karl Marx, *The Communist Manifesto* (London: Penguin, 2014).
6 Benjamin, "Capitalism and Religion," 259.
7 Ibid., 260.
8 Richard Dawson, "Fulfilment Centre," *2020*. Domino Records, 2019.
9 Katerina Paramana, "The Contemporary Dance Economy: Problems and Potentials in the Contemporary Neoliberal Moment," *Dance Research* 35, no. 1 (2017): 75–95. Quoted in: Katerina Paramana, "Performance, Dance and Political Economy: A Provocation," this volume.
10 See the etymology of "honesty" here: https://www.etymonline.com/word/honesty.

6 FEELING MY WAY THROUGH SEVERAL BEGINNINGS
Alexandrina Hemsley

(A Response to the Editors' Provocations)

We bleed we cry we leak we overflow
Time to stop fearing emotionality
Time to use it as a force
(HEMSLEY AND JOHNSON-SMALL, 2018)[1]

Do you want to get on stage? Would you like to come here?
Sit on this chair? Or over there? Or over there? In the trees?
Whose laps did we sit on? You? You? I don't remember.
My hair was in my eyes and I didn't see you.
Want a drink? What do you want?
We need you. We need you now. For the next bit.
(HEMSLEY AND JOHNSON-SMALL, 2011–13)[2]

I'd like to take our sabbatical as a starting point. I'd like to take health as a starting point. I'd like to take wonderment and survivorship as a starting point. I'd like to take devastation and freefall as a starting point. I'd like to take failure as a starting point. I'd like to take transparency as a starting point. I'd like to take dissonance as a starting point. I'd like to take misallocation of resources as a starting point. I'd like to take willfully forgotten histories as a starting point. I'd like to take giving back as a starting point. I'd like to take doubt as a starting point. I'd like to take flying and fleeing as a starting point. Stuttering, flickering, resolve. Rage, imagination, drive.

I am going to feel my way through.

Dance's communion with emotional and physical landscapes is simultaneously a turn inward to sensations and interiors and a swinging invitation outward, to meet, encounter, or guess at the sensations, needs, and interiors of others; witnesses, audiences, gazers, passersby. Within such actions and effects lies dance's potential (or perhaps illusionary) capacity to resist, through its infinitely multiple unfoldings of embodied realities, becoming wholly captured and/or commodified.[3] The scope of our embodied realities is vast, and dance seeks to engage with these threads between our physical, chemical, emotional, imaginative, and physical dimensions; encouraging an endlessness.[4]

In capitalism's time of the production of "experience," this resistance is becoming more and more risky and at risk. Or more fragile in its "realness." Dance is up for grabs. How can communication and connection touch us when everything has a look, a vibe, a predictability? Every aesthetic or action (digital, real, or as yet uncategorized) is distributed rapidly and globally as a signal of background, status, personality, and preferences.

Capitalist economies thrive by reducing and extracting the everpotent, un-fully knowable vagaries of emotional life into legible, confined messaging. This sinister handling of a body's knowledge and communication systems is overwhelming and at times feels so large that it is untraceable. Mutability is transformed into the monotony of BUY THIS STUFF. THROW IT AWAY. REPLACE WITH SHINIER, SKINNIER, LUXE STUFF. And sometimes the "stuff" is, of course, as much an idea, an aim, a performance of living, as it is an object.

Some of our London shops look like luxury hotels. Their choreography and consideration of sound, sight, smell, pathways are not intended toward supporting our bodies, but to stimulate hormones and desires toward buying a sense of subtraction (we buy one month what goes out of fashion the next, or sign up to subscriptions supposedly replenishing a need but draining our finances; a continual, deliberate, and profitable cycle of buying what we think we need and being convinced that we need more). We are meant to cultivate this lacking and participate in exchanges and environments which foster competition and pressure. We scramble for scraps. Where are the spaces to feel anything other than trapped? Or rather, where are the spaces to acknowledge the trapping—the textures that are unlikely to shift in our lifetimes—while sitting alongside other potentials for nurturing existence and creativity?

If dance proposes an excess, a useful uselessness under the frames of capitalism, a vanishing, fleeting idea and object, then perhaps it is the detecting, investing, surfacing, and expressing of dance's vibrations which always has been and always will be a political act?

This is a belief—often articulated differently across the years of a collaboration I share with Jamila Johnson-Small called Project O—which has sustained whatever we name as a shared creative practice. And yet, we could also stop. We have needed to stop. At times we are forced to stop. Our day draws to a close; a vibrant, splintering sunset.

I'd like to take the underworlds opened up by trauma as a starting point. I'd like to take tides, fog, and mist as a starting point. I'd like to take wonderment and survivorship as a starting point. I'd like to take being sexually assaulted on stage as a starting point. I'd like to take devastation and freefall as a starting point. I'd like to take the audience's titters and silence as a starting point. I'd like to take exposure as a starting point. I'd like to take lack of protection as a starting point. I'd like to take excuses as a starting point. I'd like to take willfully forgotten responsibilities as a starting point. I'd like to take flying and fleeing as a starting point. I'd like to take the careless commodification of care and consent as a starting point. Departure, censorship, hiding. Intimacy, violence, deceit.

Under capitalist economies, powerlessness is capitalized upon and the powerful are protected. Capitalism cannot handle rape but partakes in and perpetuates the events and exchanges of will, need, and power. Land, bodies, voices, ambitions, successes, imaginations. All and each violated. Overpowered. In spite of its roots and strength, a forest burns and falls.

Multiple experiences of powerlessness from sexual assaults and abuse have ruptured my biographical timeline—each one feeling like an ending. An ending of being in my body. An ending of my agency and subjecthood. They are bewildering and tragic testaments to the life-changing effects of trauma and—perhaps more uncomfortably but just as vital for understanding—evidence of the internalization of narratives of sexual violence; narratives authored by men to signal character development for female protagonists and/or ways for female subjecthood to be obliterated.[5] The drawn out consequences—one of those endings without an end—are a map to an underworld I try to coax my body out of, or at least to accept that the terrain of loss is where we are now. And so we need to commence the hunt for imagery and voice. I ask myself without words—more like muscular articulations—can dance be a way through this? Not out of. I have no desire to get out of anything. I will not reject a landscape emerged by trauma—individual or collective, personal or systemic—for it is mine and I've spent too long trying to belong to external places. I may as well try and belong to myself.

Stuttering, flickering, resolve. Rage, imagination, drive.

In January 2020, I turned my writing practice toward these ideas of retrieving the parts which disappeared in a stranger's hands or the disconnections forced upon my sense of self within the operations of white, supremacist, ableist patriarchy. The violence of power and abuse are described as an evaporation of sorts:

> the water around her ran cold
> over toes that did not touch the bottom of the sand bed
> she was treading water
>
> she was enveloped
> she calmly, painfully vanished.[6]

At a later point, after many years, a retrieval begins:

> Now as I visit the past, I am hoping to leave a little less of myself trapped there each time.
>
> A 33-year-old is diving back in time to help fight that man off and keep hold of the eleven-year-old girl's edges. When she arrives, the eleven-year-old is already mid-vanish, losing parts of herself to the water. Surrendering her soul-life overboard. Weeping edges; internal rhythms which know they are losing parts of themselves. The surrounding waters become sites of violence, disappearance, and sanctuary.
>
> She does not cry. There is already so much water.
>
> The older woman casts her arms wide as a fishing net, encasing the half-girl. Their skin membranes melt, and the woman absorbs the girl. All the parts we thought were lost, crystallise in her bloodstream. They no longer need to flee.

Her blood begins the process of repair of her younger panicked fragments. Calming the jumbled, disorientated voices. The younger finally reassembles. The older's bones bend in empathy.[7]

🍄 🍄 🍄 🍄 🍄 🍄 🍄 🍄

In 2018, Project O proposed adopting the model of a sabbatical for the Live Art Development Agency's *Diverse Actions Leadership Bursary*. We were going to withdraw and pause our practice as Project O as a way of investing in a regathering of energies and responding critically to the models of "leadership" which frequently expect and pressurize Black artists to assimilate our modalities into the language and attitudes of success under white supremacist, capitalist patriarchy. Jamila and I wrote:

> We wanted to approach this bursary application with integrity, thinking about what our needs really are right now in relationship to ideas of leadership, support, care, development, growth and ideas of future shifting of power structures and visioning and mobilisation of new models. **How can we think ahead if we have never thought about now?** We are so constantly encouraged—whilst attempting to make live work—to consider the future and the past but what about the present, this moment, these moments and how we exist in them Now? Beyond anticipation and the lenses of precarity that make time something that chases . . . (emphasis in original)

Project O want to go on sabbatical. Academics get one year for every seven they have worked, we can go with 4 months and fees of £1,250 per month.

How can we value ourselves, our bodies and our work, and not think first about redistribution of funds or how to maximise a grant, increase the scale of a project? What if ambition is not bigger, larger, more but actually respecting our process and taking ourselves seriously. So often the way "respect" or "admiration" is shown in the sector is through processes that deplete our resources, we are generous, we do give, so can we trust this and take a moment to breathe?

How can art practice not spiral inwards?

We wanted to engage in:

> Refreshing the relevance of practice.
> Consuming engulfing structures of the artworld.
> Re-thinking ideas of "production" and productiveness.
> Considering boundaries between the people and the work.
> What happens when there is a gap? What is in a gap? What is a gap?
> Considering the various interconnected structures that we live inside of and in relation and these systems of influence and replication—is there a way to do process before imagining and pre-designing a product?
> How do we assign value to art objects and practices? Who are the current leaders? Who is following them? Why?
> What happens when we stop?
> How do we accept that what we do is make art and that to stop this will be an enforced and repressive action.
> What is refusal and when is it radical? Is a pause a refusal?"

We didn't get the grant.

But, we did get a discretionary grant to have a sabbatical from the partner organization. Maybe we would have felt more effective with the visibility of the grant? Maybe we preferred the privacy of the discretionary grant? Maybe we benefited from conversations behind closed doors. Maybe we failed in the fight for greater representation?

We took the discretionary grant.

We paused Project O. In many ways, we are still pausing Project O and tracing in private the ways our collaboration continues to hold and shift in relation to our creativity and wider engagements with living.

I'd like to take kinship as a starting point. I'd like to take tides, fog, and mist as a starting point. I'd like to take wonderment and survivorship as a starting point. I'd like to take working for nearly a decade with the same person as a starting point. I'd like to take perseverance and freefall as a starting point. I'd like to take our aging as a starting point. I'd like to take exposure as a starting point. I'd like to take lack of protection as a starting point. I'd like to take sharing stories as a starting point. I'd like to take sifting through market pressure and market bullshit as a starting point. I'd like to take unpaid meetings as a starting point. I'd like to take the careless commodification of care and consent as a starting point. Overdrafts, censorship, shame. Shudders, shyness, re-embodiment.

Notes

1 *X* 2018, [program text of live performance] Choreographers Alexandrina Hemsley and Jamila Johnson-Small.

2 *O* 2011-13, [audio from live performance] Choreographers Alexandrina Hemsley and Jamila Johnson-Small.

3 Tapping into our hidden emotional lives, imaginations, and visualizations during dancing is one of the ways dance resists capture.

4 For example, the unfolding process of dance improvisation offers up both explicit visuals (what an audience sees) and opaque offerings (why did the dance arrive there in that moment? What might the dancer have been feeling?). Often and importantly, the sensations guiding the dancer are hidden. The work of choreography could be choosing what to expose and what to keep private, while also ensuring the dancer is in an environment (staging, lighting, costume, and sound choices) that is in a continual flux of supporting, championing, and protecting their performing.

5 Rajeswan Sander Rajan's essay "Life after Rape; Narrative, Rape and Feminism" offers a moving, detailed, and thoughtful critique of these narrative tropes; particularly in canonical English novels. Rajeswan Sander Rajan, "Life After Rape; Narrative, Rape and Feminism," in *Real and Imagined Women: Gender, Culture and Postcolonialism* (New York: Routledge, 1993), 61–78.

6 I performed a reading of these texts on the invitation of Florence Peake to accompany her work *Cave* (2020). The night was part of *Hyper Functional, Ultra Healthy* festival at Somerset House, London, January 30, 2020.

7 Ibid.

DIALOGUE 3
REST, PRODUCTIVITY AND SURVIVAL

Mark Arthur, in "Sleepwalking: Toward a New Corporeality of Dance," draws attention to the tensions between rest, embodiment, temporality, and race, which he suggests are connected by "an oppressive investment in sleep" and an increasing demand for productivity. Johnson-Small's chapter "It Only Happens in Daylight" is a performance on paper about productivity despite the need for rest. She connects these ideas to the political and socioeconomic context and to race. In Dialogue 3, each author reflects on the demands of political economy on bodies, and the possibilities that emerge for other ways of moving in the contemporary productivity-driven world.

7 SLEEPWALKING
TOWARD A NEW CORPOREALITY OF DANCE
Marc Arthur

(A Response to the Editors' Provocations)

The rise of the free-market economy increasingly makes people conceive of themselves as self-managing enterprises in every facet of life. In what follows, I suggest that this phenomenon can be witnessed in two works, *Tickle the Sleeping Giant* (by Trajal Harrell) and *Black Power Naps* (by Nivald Acosta and Fannie Sosa), which examine movement in its most innate state—unconscious sleeping bodies. What emerges are tensions between rest, embodiment, race, and temporality that are tied together by an oppressive investment in sleep and supported by an ever-escalating demand for economic productivity. I begin by providing some context through a discussion of the theory of economic self-management as articulated by Michel Foucault. I also cover a brief history of artists who have made sleep central to their practice. Then I examine and analyze how *Tickle the Sleeping Giant* and *Black Power Naps* highlight and contest the economic and political management of sleep.

In his lectures on *The Birth of Biopolitics*, Foucault draws on a genealogy of political thought and texts primarily from German post–Second World War reformation to put forward the idea that emerging economic policies at the time were key to building the modern liberal state. These new forms of governmentality incentivized small- and medium-sized enterprises that avoided centralization.[1] In opposition to the command economy of the Soviet Union and of the authoritarian Nazi regime, this new economy forced subjects and social bodies to step up, compensate, and take responsibility for their own economic management in all areas of social life. Foucault articulates this as a society that is both active and passive in its economic control, "a society for the market and a society against the market, a society oriented towards the market and a society that compensates for the effects of the market in the realm of values and existence."[2] Implemented directly after the Second World War as a way to produce and legitimate a new West Germany, this economic logic, according to Foucault, has been the main structuring device that led to the country's successful economic reconstruction as a new liberal state. This is more or less how he understands neoliberalism—the methodologies by which human conduct is organized and directed by the free market within the state in a generalized form.[3]

Key to his analysis is that the new economic imperatives and enterprises extend beyond the economy to the social body and individual subjects, to the "realm of values and existence," suggesting that "monetary exchanges function in American neo-liberalism as a principle of intelligibility and a principle of decipherment of social relationships and individual behavior."[4] Here, Foucault is referring to the ways in which the market seeps into behavior and becomes a principle of knowledge and self-conception by which other parts of life outside of the economy function. While his theory does not name the human body specifically as a site of intelligibility, Foucault's theory of economics is relevant to embodied experiences as they are intimately tied to social behaviors and self-conceptualization.

Looking to the history of performance art since the 1960s, a number of works come to mind that frame sleep as an artistic encounter and expose it as a site of political contestation. Perhaps most famous is Chris Burden's *Bed Piece* (1972), which consisted of a gallery with only a bed on which the artist slept for twenty-two days without leaving. In an interview, Burden reflects on how this piece is perhaps stranger and more violent than his more well-known and dramatic works, like "Shoot" (1971) in which he was shot in the arm.[5] Other works which stand out include Techching Hsieh's *One Year Performance* (1978–9) in which the artist spent a year locked in a cage in the Museum of Modern Art, or Marina Abramović's *House with an Ocean View* (2002), a piece where the artist lived in a gallery for a week sleeping, bathing, and eating. These works—all of which were created and presented in the context of visual art—offer precedents that disclose the theatricalization of everyday activities, which includes sleep. For the purposes of this chapter, I am more interested in what is at stake for choreographers who conceptualize sleep in their work, particularly because dancers tend to be more intimately engaged with examining how economic power is inscribed in their bodies.

Choreographer Trajal Harrell's performance series *Tickle the Sleeping Giant* (2001–12) was staged in galleries and theaters and consisted of two to ten dancers sleeping on large white foam mats in typical dance practice attire. Each approximately eight-hour performance took place in a raw space and spectators came and left as they wished. Harrell's instructions were that dancers take the sleeping drug Ambien at the start of the performance and sleep until the effects of the drug wore off. By giving his dancer's Ambien, Harrell was interested, in part, in how his dancers' bodies are moved and capitalized on by the pharmaceutical industry's management of sleep.

In his book *24/7 Late Capitalism and the Ends of Sleep*, Jonathan Crary suggests that over the course of the twentieth century, sleep became understood, along with other necessities of human life including hunger, thirst, sexual, desires, and friendship, as being at odds with the voraciousness of contemporary capitalism.[6] Biomedical methods of sleep management emerged in postwar America and Europe in tandem with the rise of neoliberalism, the same period Foucault describes techniques for self-optimization coming to prominence.[7] For Crary, sleep is the last frontier of the total economic management of human behavior as it confounds the market with a profound way of being outside of time and, as such, may in fact pose the greatest threat of all to the forward march of capitalism—sleep is when we spend the most out of sync from endless circulations of production and consumption. As sleeping medications like Ambien seek to prevent insomnia, they imbue a market logic into sleeping bodies insofar as a restful night of sleep is an investment in future productivity. In Harrell's dance, spectators witness this process live. That is, they engage in a theatrical encounter with dancers who perform the effects of Ambien live, and thus reveal the effect of the drug's economic imperative—of the economic clock of production—on their bodies. Watching Harrell's dancers highlights how the time of sleep has been reorganized by the regularization of profitability, of industrial time. As they try to sleep in the bright lights of a theater or gallery, it also becomes apparent how sleep has been altered by artificial lighting, and more recently by the new 24/7 digital economy.

André Lepecki, who curated *Tickle the Sleeping Giant* as part of a program at the Haus der Kulturen der Welt in Berlin (2009), writes that Harrell was less a choreographer and more of a caretaker or attendant. Lepecki describes how Harrell watched each performer closely, making sure that spectators did not disrupt the dancers and that he could protect them if they experienced any of the drug's side-effects, such as somnambulism (sleep walking).[8] Lepecki's analysis also reveals another choreographer of the piece: Ambien. The dancers' techniques and movements were organized by the effects of the drug, and in turn they performed its pharmacological choreography as they writhed and jostled. As dancers lost physical agency and moved to the drug's effects, they danced to the meter and music of self-optimizing economic management, of a 24/7 culture, in which there is no time for sleep, and we must always be "on."

Under neoliberalism, the implicit expectation that individuals take responsibility for their own economic management works differently for people who exist within conditions of structural inequality. The pharmaceutical market, for example, privileges those of a certain class who have access to or can afford healthcare and sleeping medications. Economies of sleep also take specifically racialized forms. Consider how multiple studies have shown a sleep gap in which People of Color get five times less sleep than white people.[9] These studies reveal that People of Color not only get fewer hours of sleep per night but also get lower levels of the restorative "slow-wave" sleep as a result of longer hours of work and the constant discrimination which makes it difficult to relax.[10]

These studies are at the center of queer Afro Latinx artists Navild Acosta's and Fannie Sosa's *Black Power Naps*, which they have staged at performance venues across Europe and the United States since 2018. At Performance Space in New York in 2019, the piece consisted of both an installation and a series of live "activations" with movement, song, and text. Seven elaborate, cozy, and decadent "healing" stations were installed in the venue's black box theater. Some meditative, others more eccentric, these napping spaces were created with hammocks, mattresses, black beans, cushions, and a waterbed. They were adorned with shimmering curtains, lavender scented blankets, mood lighting, and some included subwoofers that emitted a low relaxing hum. In press materials and in the program, People of Color were invited to come and relax, rest, and sleep:

> *Black Power Naps* is a direct response to the Sleep Gap, which the artists see as a continued form of state-sanctioned punishment born from the ongoing legacy of slavery. Reclaiming idleness and play as sources of power and strength, this installation takes over Performance Space's large theater and invites people of color to break with constant fatigue by slowing down, resting, and interacting with soft, comfortable surfaces.[11]

In connecting the sleep gap to ongoing legacies of slavery, their piece highlights how contemporary economics prolong historical violence in the present, as evidenced by the deficient conditions of sleep for People of Color.

Having presented their work at contemporary dance spaces for many years, Acosta and Sosa were interested not only in revealing the racialized ways in which sleep has been economized, but in highlighting how such a process is mirrored in the economics of performance venues, which implicitly ask People of Color to self-optimize and perform their race for the public. In the program for their performance they also write, "Our culture has required that People of Color present themselves as extraordinary performers, athletes, or entertainers in order to exist in the public realm. *Black Power Naps* refuses institutionalized exhaustion and demands the redistribution of idleness, down time, and quality sleep."[12] If there is an expectation that artists of color constantly be "on," that they are constantly asked to perform racial difference, *Black Power Naps* responds by envisioning and building a space where the central motivation of performance is the act of sleep.

A vinyl text piece on the floor of their installation reads, "If you see a black person resting, don't call the police!" This tongue and cheek message not only resists processes by which aesthetic evaluations of Black bodies result in violence, but also alludes to how a performance venue might inadvertently echo such processes through audience/performer interactions. As a white person, I never used the space. And I was highly aware of my presence in the installation as I walked through, even if the few people resting in the space were not aware of me. This was the point of the performance: to challenge the presumed whiteness of performing arts institutions and to highlight prevalent white surveillance practices that potentially inform the quality of sleep for People of Color.

I was also struck by the artist's evocation of a queer sense of time, and how this played a role in disrupting economies of racialized insomnia. The Atlantic Reconciliation Station, for example, was constructed with shimmering fabric and a neon tie-dyed bed spread. It looked like the perfect napping site for one of the queer performance artist Nick Cave's fabulously eccentric sound suit performers. A photograph hanging above the waterbed in the installation pictured a group of people, some of whom appeared to be gender nonconforming, wearing rhinestones, brightly colored makeup, and glittery outfits. The installation evoked what Tavia Nyong'o has described as Black polytemporality that is queer insofar as it "resists reproductive, developmental, and accumulative time, but also insofar as it is availed to an array of incompossible subjects that must each find it at their own tempo."[13] The space was designed precisely so that People of Color could dance and rest at their own tempo. It urged a polytemporality of sleep, which saturates outside modes of economized and racialized sleep that are centered on the exploitation of productivity with a sense of play. Dreaming was perhaps most present during the hour-long loop of Caribbean lullabies, Black science fiction, and subliminal programming that played softly in the background. This soundtrack also featured the artists reading an ASMR-style manifesto on Black leisure, joy, play, pleasure, and sleep, which in turn subtly conjured a hopeful futurity. The installation created a polytemporality that disrupted the economic organization of time and calibrated a space not only of rest but also of dreaming.

The most significant and intriguing difference between Harrell's *Sleeping Giant* and Acosta and Sosa's *Black Power Naps* is the latter's invitation to dream. In Harrel's dance, sleep is expressed at a comatose and inert Ambien-induced tempo and spectators are asked to observe sleeping dancers. To the contrary, in *Black Power Naps* white audience spectatorship is linked to the surveillance of People of Color and to the racial exploitation of sleep. In their effort to resist this exploitation, Acosta and Sosa build undisturbed and tranquil stations, where bright colors and interactive materials seek to achieve a radical form of sleep that inspires new dreams. These differences, of course, stem from the artists' respective motivating questions regarding the ways pharmaceutical and racist economies affect sleeping bodies. Be it Harrell's invitation to spectators to consider the economic imperatives of Ambien by watching drugged sleeping dancers, or Acosta and Sosa's emphasis on the manner in which legacies of sleep-deprived racial capitalism inform dance created by artists of color, both artists reveal how economic control is embedded in bodies and offer clues for how to move and dance differently against such forces. Put another way, they use choreography as a corrective to the regulation of corporeality. This regulation is what Foucault describes as a "cost of time, and therefore an economic cost,"[14] and which is applied to every aspect of social relations and individual behavior.

*

Tickle the Sleeping Giant and *Black Power Naps* offer different modes and methods for dance to expose or de-sync from market-driven relationships to time. In doing so, both works provide instructive examples of how dance reveals the manner in which, as Anita Gonzalez notes, "interventions in the macros of political economies begin in the micro,"[15] and how, as Katerina Paramana proposes, exploring "the relation between performance/dance and political economy . . . can contribute to imagining a world beyond the present."[16]

Harrell achieves this, in part, through his dancers' movement vocabulary—stark, spasmodic, or even still—which exhibits a pharmaceutical temporality of sleep: sleep premised on future productivity and regularity. His dancers' style of movement has led me to wonder whether the extraordinary preoccupation with managing sleep might also contribute to a glossary of movement in contemporary dance that looks like sleepwalking, especially in works like *Sylphides* by Cecilia Bengolea and François Chaignaud (2008), *Agape* by FlucT (2012), *Faust* by Anne Imhof (2017), and site specific performances by Young Boy Dancing Group (2019). In addition, dancers in all of the pieces that I just mentioned exhibit lugubrious detachment in their gestures and pacing, their gaze and attitudes are overcome with Brechtian alienation taken to its most convoluted extreme. And yet, this choreographic trend also risks participating in economic calendars that demand production, particularly as many of these performances have been presented by museums and galleries that inadvertently situate dancing bodies in the context of value systems of art collection. Acosta and Sosa intentionally create choreography that resists the economic imperatives of commissioning performance, particularly as they are manifested along racial lines and result in performers of color who are overworked and tired. Rather than dance that swells with exhaustion, *Black Power Naps* reminds us that perhaps the most political effect of conceptualizing dance and sleep together is the activation of dreaming as a critical practice. Sleep is something everyone needs. Dance, like sleep, is corporeal and provides a window into uncharted experiences of time. As sleep is increasingly carved apart by the never-ending greed of productivity and becomes more and more regulated and contained by processes of self-optimization, dance can provide examples of what it would look and feel like to purposefully step outside the regime of profit-earning time, and to dream of other ways of moving.

Notes

1 Michel Foucault, *The Birth of Biopolitics: Lectures at the Collège De France*, trans. Michel Senellart (Basingstoke: Palgrave Macmillan, [1978–79] 2008), 240.

2 Ibid., 242.

3 Ibid.

4 Ibid., 243.

5 *Chris Burden Documented Projects 71–74* (1975), [film] Dir. Chris Burden, https://vimeo.com/29168858#t=552. Citation for "Bed Piece," Market Street Program (1972), min. 9:13.

6 Jonathan Crary, *24/7 Late Capitalism and the Ends of Sleep* (London: Verso, 2013), 10.

7 Foucault, *The Birth of Biopolitics,* 10.

8 This and preceding sentence from André Lepecki, "Moving as Thing: Choreographic Critiques of the Object," *October* 140 (2012): 75–90, 82.

9 Brian Resnick, "The Black-White Sleep Gap," *The Atlantic* (October 23): https://www.theatlantic.com/politics/archive/2015/10/the-black-white-sleep-gap/454311/

10 Ibid.

11 Fannie Sosa and Nivald Acosta, "Program Note, 'In Our Society,'" *Broadly* (January 2019), 2.

12 Ibid.

13 Tavia Nyong'o, *Afro-Fabulations: The Queer Drama of Black Life* (New York: NYU Press, 2018), 11.

14 Foucault, *The Birth of Biopolitics,* 245.

15 Anita Gonzalez, "Recognizing Race and Class in Dance: Gonzalez Response to Paramana," this volume.

16 Katerina Paramana, "Performance, Dance and Political Economy: A Provocation," this volume.

8 IT ONLY HAPPENS IN DAYLIGHT
Jamila Johnson-Small

(A Response to the Editors' Provocations)

Key

1.

I don't mind making a fool out of myself over you. / Well, I mind. I feel embarrassed for you.[1]

2.

Loiter[2]

- to stand or wait around without apparent purpose.
- to walk slowly with no apparent purpose.
- the act of remaining in a particular public place for a protracted time without apparent purpose.
- a preceding offense to other forms of public crime and disorder.

3.

Sun hits my neck, softly.

Note, that it is not okay to be without visible purpose.

Everything should have a function. Purpose should be explicit, legible, and announced.[3]

Introduction

I am thinking about the relationship between performance and advertising, packaging and dissemination of ideology, building of brands and empires and subcultures.... The hunger for performance—to experience it, to host it, to present it, to discuss it—feels particularly invasive right now. I have been writing to P____ about making work like Trojan horses, things that look and articulate in the ways that I know these people and institutions want to be excited, things that are really about something else and for other purposes that do not get shared explicitly or are maybe not visible as distinct from what is outwardly proposed. Things keep circling around the words "devastation" and "sabotage."

Text

Last night I wanted to cry so much I thought that I would be broken, a puddle, a body of water, forever incapable.

-

Frameworks gripped tight in the name of survival.

-

No line is straight.

-

Time and sensation are opiates of the imaginary and when order-sign-symptom is no longer attributed, some kind of gentle hell shakes itself loose.

-

I think that I am trying to say something about the mad intimacy of dancing as it upsets all perceived boundaries, and its own.

-

Any frame brings some form of order and establishes some kind of legibility.

-

This cannot work.

-

The feeling is that I am asked to betray myself, again and again, in order to make space for that self.

-

I do not want to say that I am at any intersection—I am not a street, not a city, not a juncture, not a meeting place.

-

Economies demand that on some level there is agreement about value.

-

I want to give this space.

-

The beginning of the conversation already contained everything we need to know and want to talk about.

-

There was no proposed fee in the initial approach for us (Project O) to contribute to this publication, because it was forgotten that we—as freelance artists—do not have a salary.

-

A question about terrain, a question about desire and relation.

-

A sign post.

-

Today, I hope to be a stick in the mud.

-

Something that is not kettling.

-

And the object is to move, in/side relation.

-

This is where I am moved.

-

The value is in the poetry of the gesture.

-

Here, between vows and a manifesto, testifying.

-

Truth is, I have only eaten a tube of paprika crisps and drunk a flask of green tea today, my cunt feels a bit raw from morning fucking and the sun hits me on my left side.

-

The offence to order, the confusion, the disruption, the anxiety.

-

The impossibility of living while Black.

-

[I do not give these words any meaning of my own, they are more fabrications bred from reasoning that has never been mine]

-

As I write this, I am wondering if it makes any sense to you and I am thinking about the proximities between Blackness and insanity.

-

The problem is, I will miss you.

-

I know it has been suggested before.

-

Maybe we should stop speaking.

-

We keep circling around the need for rest, the urgency for less productivity, imbibing what is toxic in order to gain the means to shout louder, last longer, and to fight more voraciously.

-

To do so would make me a hypocrite in relation to the invitation.

-

I thought about watching all of those videos but I didn't.

-

But we haven't spoken about it and maybe you don't want all those people coming in.

-

Sometimes you turn my shoes the other way around and I want to tell you that, as I understand it, the energy is better with the toes pointing in and not away, the flow of the rising of the shoes as the fabric reaches for the ankle is another barrier.

-

We have never spoken about it but there is this thing where you leave the shoes by the wall with toes pointing outward, and I leave the shoes with toes directed in.

-

You will always reorganize everything that I say however it is that you want.

-

// refrain //

-

And so it follows—this has always been about you.

\-

I don't want to and I have been told many times that I only do what I want.

\-

My mind becomes a spreadsheet and there are some thrills attached to this, the titillation and disappointment of seeing behind the scenes.

\-

I am tired of seeing money and equations—data—when I am looking at performance.

\-

There is only movement and nothing that has been done can be undone and I am working to work less, not to have an abstract conversation about labor, exchange, and use-value.

\-

My job is to make sexy sentences that allow people to imagine some moments of relief.

\-

To do this, you have to think that you know something about who you are talking to.

\-

I am a salesman.

\-

We deal in artifice to make vessels to contain surplus feeling, because what can be done with feeling (other than dancing?)?

\-

The disappearance of performance from the time and place it happened is a relief, always.

\-

Oppositional forces perpetuate one another.

\-

I want to think about the impossibility of beginnings and endings with you.

-

Do we need a marker that says, "The End"?

-

Do we (I) need structure?

-

-

I wonder if it is possible to do it without following the arc of climax, the work of the adrenal glands?

-

It is beautiful and stupid to make performance.

-

Excuses and reasons are found through processes of fabrication—they are not t/here.

-

touching me touching you touching me touching you touching me touching you touching me touching you touching me touching you touching me touching you touching me touching you touching me touching you

-

This has always been about You.

-

... the linear narrativizing and historicizing of everything ...

-

Your arms around my waist, on the pads of fat that precede my hips, those hands, their form, their pressure ... they made me.

-

I know that you are looking for somebody to hold you, I am too.

Prophet, oracle, administrator . . .

\-

Hustler, magician, service provider, body that can and will endure the violence of being looked at.

\-

One of the questions is, what would be the minimal number of instructions needed to bring something into being?

\-

It happens only in daylight.

\-

I will not save you.

\-

This is not a study, nor an analysis, nor a manifesto—that would be someone else's job.

\-

There are no answers and everything changes with/in/over time.

\-

Art will not save you and you are always alone, don't let the darkness or the sweetness fool you.

\-

Art will not save you.

\-

I think that the title of this thing will be *I Don't Mind Making a Fool of Myself over You.*

\-

This text is my proposition for an upcoming performance commission.

\-

It will become itself.

Or it will resist.

-

Or it will transform.

-

I don't like to think of this as a transaction but this language becomes me, like your saliva when we kiss, the smells of you lying next to me in the morning; shaped by proximity, this body will assimilate.

-

All of your words are actions on my body, fantasies on my mind.

-

I think.

-

Soon.

-

I will leave again.

-

Everything that I will say here is bound up in time, this time, these constellations of relation—you led me here.

Notes

1 From memory of the exchange between Margaret and Brick in the film production of Tennessee William's play *Cat on a Hot Tin Roof* (1955). Actual quote from the film is:

> Margaret: I don't mind making a fool of myself over you.
>
> Brick: I mind, Maggie. I feel embarrassed for you. (Act II, 32).

Cat on a Hot Tin Roof, DVD, Metro-Goldwyn-Mayer, Los Angeles, 1958.

2 Fragments extrapolated from the Wikipedia definition for "loitering" (https://en.wikipedia.org/wiki/Loitering).

3 My words.

DIALOGUE 4
COMMUNAL DISRUPTIONS

Melissa Blanco Borelli's "Community, Coloniality and Convivencia in the Festival de Danza de Santa María la Antigua del Darién, Colombia" discusses a region in Colombia, in which communities were able to "re-member and re-choreograph themselves back into the(ir) space after histories of displacement" by staging and performing in a festival. Usva Seregina's "Changing Our Bodies' Relationships to Reality," a response to Bojana Cvejić and Christine de Smedt's performance *Spatial Confessions* and Christian Falsnaes's *FORCE* from the video playlist, examines the ways existing normative structures might be disrupted by deconstructing familiar relationships of one's body to space. Dialogue 4 offers insights into communities and discusses ways that engaging with performance/dance allows for the critique of the past and of the present and can help forge new futures and politico-economic models.

9 COMMUNITY, COLONIALITY AND *CONVIVENCIA* IN THE FESTIVAL DE DANZA DE SANTA MARÍA LA ANTIGUA DEL DARIÉN, COLOMBIA

Melissa Blanco Borelli

(A Response to the Editors' Provocations)

> "It is crucial that we embark on a new political economy project; one that affords us the opportunity to change 'our relation to work, transform our noetic processes (processes of perceiving and processing information/ thinking), and **enhance our capacity for being with others.**'" Katerina Paramana (my emphasis)[1]

This research was funded by the Arts and Humanities Research Council (Embodied Performance Practices AH/R013748/1) and information was gathered in collaboration with Anamaría Tamayo Duque, Marta Dominguez Mejía, and Isabel Restrepo Jaramillo. We thank the community members cited in this chapter for their generosity of time, knowledge, and spirit.

"Yet the streets, the clubs and *other quotidian spaces* nurture all kinds of dancing; **dancing where different cultural codes are at work.**"
Anita Gonzalez[2]

Prologue

In June 2019, a dance festival took place at the ruins of Dariena (now known as Santa María la Antigua del Darién), the first mainland settlement in the Americas in present-day Colombia. Conquistador Vasco Núñez de Balboa founded Dariena in 1501. By 1524 Balboa was dead, Panamá City had become imperial Spain's main priority in that geographical location, and local Indigenous communities burned down what was left of Dariena. Eventually, one of the first *palenques* (Black fugitive communities) of Africans emerged nearby, and by the nineteenth century, these lands were settled by free Blacks and *cimarrones* (fugitives).[3] The dance festival, which enacted a historical trajectory of displacement as a result of colonialism, took place after lunchtime. Each community presented their dances: the Guna Tule Indigenous community from Arquía presented their dance called *La Zeta* (the Zed); the Embera community from the Eyaquera territory presented the dances *La Paloma* (the dove) and *La Guacamaya* (the parrot); the Afro-Colombian community from Marriaga danced the *mapalé*; the women and girls from the Citará Indigenous community danced *La Arriera*; the Afro-Colombian dance group from Unguía's Casa de Cultura performed the *Abozao del Pacífico*; and the women and girls from the Embera Cuti community presented their dances *El Pato* (the duck) and *La Rana* (the frog).

In this chapter, I turn to two community and/or cultural leaders who led some of the dance events that afternoon in June 2019. Through their specific relationships to dance, heritage, land, and their communities, I want to highlight *how* the act of converging over the ground that bears the (im)material, yet still palpable, remnants of coloniality and state violence choreographs *convivencia* at this gathering. I see *convivencia*, the ability to coexist, in this case, through a dance performance, as a confluence of dance and political economy. The minimal institutional support via the Colombian state's renewed interest in the region enables the communities to re-member and re-choreograph themselves back into the(ir) space after histories of displacement. *Convivencia* becomes a mode by which these communities can respond to the colonial repertoires of the state and inscribe new meanings to a violent past and present. More importantly, *convivencia* demonstrates their ability to continually coexist despite the afterlives of colonialism and the Colombian armed conflict, a conflict that affects them but, ironically, has nothing do to with them.

Setting the Scene: Unguía, Urabá, Chocó, and the Colombian Armed Conflict

A rich history of colonial disdain and disavowal rests uneasily over the landscape here in the northern Chocó/Urabá region of the Colombian department of Antioquia; it is a landscape dotted by banana and rubber trees and cattle, and adorned by the ornate tributaries of brown sediment-strewn rivers and their corresponding streams.[4] The geopolitical location of Unguía, one of the larger municipalities in this northern region of the Chocó department in Colombia (and next to the Urabá region), has made it a focal point of the government's transcontinental capitalist megaprojects.[5] The region became a site where the multifarious interests of capitalist organizations, oligarchic elites, right-wing paramilitary groups, left-wing guerrillas, the government, and the military led to a large majority of displacements among the populations who lived in the area: Indigenous and Afro-Colombian communities. More than 600 families were displaced from 1985 to 1994 under the guise of agrarian reform while the Colombian state established a new constitution in 1991 and the *Ley 70* of 1993 in order to legitimize territorial land rights for Afro-Colombians and Indigenous communities. Colombia, enacting what Giorgio Agamben would call the spectacular state, seemed to both legitimize these new Black and Indigenous "states" while simultaneously erasing their possibility of proper sovereignty due to the state's inability to protect them.[6] This discursive recognition of Afro-Colombian and Indigenous territorial sovereignty by the Colombian state further heightened the armed conflict in the Urabá region. Sovereignty in this sense harkens to Achille Mbembe's conceptualization of "necropower" and its relationship to the Fanonian colonial state, where the state has "the capacity to define who matters and who does not, who is *disposable* and who is not."[7] Coloniality suffocates Colombia and necropower exists as a script the country's conflicting factions rehearse daily. The impact of displacement and the ability to be able to return and reclaim ancestral land by literally dancing on it makes the dance festival even more significant.

Many communities still remain under siege by oligarchic landowning elites' desires for expansion, ongoing presence of paramilitary operations, extractivist multinational corporate interests, and the afterlives of political violence.[8] After the signing of the Colombian peace accords in 2016, Unguía was set up as a priority for the Justicia Especial por la Paz (JEP), a governmental institution that looks after transitional justice and peace initiatives. Other organizations such as the Truth Commission, la Unidad de Restitución de Tierra, the Centro Nacional de Memoria Histórica, and the Ministry of Culture have set the municipality of Unguía as a priority region post-conflict. Part of that prioritization involved the establishment of the Archaeological and Historic Park and Museum of Santa María de Belén la Antigua del Darién. With the support of the Ministry of Culture via the ICANH (the Colombian Institute of Anthropology and History), the government inaugurated the park in April 2019.[9] Important to reiterate is that this is an area of displaced Afro-Colombians and Indigenous communities. Some have returned. Bringing them together for a dance festival seemed like a moment to pause, breathe, and be together.

A local Unguía woman, Mónica Castro, works as the program coordinator at the park. She has held that position for about three years. Her involvement in the development of the park rests on the fact that *both* the communities and the paramilitaries—who still have a strong presence in the region—trust her.[10] The dance festival, inaugurated in June 2019, emerged from the community's desire to "rescue the cultural activities that are being lost or are no longer practiced," she says, "in order to find a way for them to strengthen these traditions or this culture that they have." For the purpose of the festival, Mónica helped organize a committee of ideas and proposals with all of the communities at the level of the municipality. About twenty-two community leaders participated and agreed upon the themes: a day of dance, a day of storytelling, and a day of sport. They wanted three events a year of which the dance festival was the first one.

Staging Community and *Convivencia*

What does it mean for these Afro-Colombians, Guna Dule, Embera Cuti, and Eyaquera communities to dance together one Saturday afternoon? How might this event generate multiple activities of memory making? And, lastly, how might dance help foster a *convivencia* (coexistence) in this fraught geopolitical landscape?

Private, public, and institutional economies are conterminous here, representative of the many afterlives of the political economy of colonialism. For example, the state attempts to incentivize the communities with the promise of a tourist economy. However these promises come laden with neoliberal models of tourism, which do not take into account the cosmologies of the communities or their relationship to and care for the environment. Furthermore, the need for economic sustainability for many of the artistic community members is often seen as a political after-thought. If they are not supported by the Ministry of Culture, cultural initiatives in these poor, rural communities are nonexistent.

Afro-Colombian dancer and choreographer Omar Mendoza often feels stifled creatively because civic support in the form of money from the *Casa de Cultura* to help fund his choreographies is inconsistent. He dreams of having a steady flow of resources to properly costume his dancers because for him, a dance is only as good as the costumes worn. Although Unguía has both a library and a *Casa de Cultura* (an office that receives funding from the Ministry of Culture for cultural events), resources are scarce. For Omar, support for cultural activity can be traced to Mauricio Vélez, a former director of the *Casa*. Before him, there was nothing. The recent mayor supports dance initiatives and when we spoke with Omar he shared that stagings of dances from the Atlantic region, the Pacific, and urban music are underway. He has an Africanist inspired choreography from 2016 that mimics the gestures and movements of eight desert animals, but he laments the inability to have proper costumes to be able to fully stage it. The fact that all of the original dancers from that production have left Unguía further curtails his creative drive. As part of his vocational dance training, Omar studied with the Guna Tule Indigenous community in the reservation of Arquía for six months.[11] In order to do this, the director of his school had to send a letter to the Indigenous leaders asking their permission for access so that Omar could partake in their dances and rituals as practices of *convivencia*, or coexistence. What does it mean to practice coexistence at a dance festival? What kinds of economies of sociality emerge from these practices at a microcultural scale tainted by territorial displacement, from the afterlife of political violence, and from cultural differences choreographed by the dancing bodies? The afterlife of political violence is what Macarena Gómez-Barris defines as "the continuing and persistent symbolic and material effects of the original event of violence on people's daily lives, their social and psychic identities, and their ongoing wrestling with the past in the present."[12] Sociality, then, through artistic practices offers a space to re-exist. It becomes a response to these multiple afterlives of violence and colonialism. By dancing their respective traditional heritages, the Indigenous and Afro communities in Unguía choreograph opportunities to come together again.

Throughout our initial conversation with Omar Mendoza, it became clear that, for him, dance and choreography cannot exist completely without financial support from the Casa de Cultura, the mayoral office, or any other governmental or corporate entity. He sees dance as dependent on—as in most free-market capitalist economies—corporate funding or minimum state funding. However, financial needs notwithstanding, his knowledge and practice of *convivencia* allow him to consistently maintain a creative presence in Unguía.

Unlike Omar Mendoza, María Guasapura, the governor of the Embera Cuti reservation and singer/dance teacher for the Embera group, does not lament anything. In fact, her only complaint is that the men in her community are cowards because they do not like to dance. To be fair, her community is matrifocal, regardless of the number of men. Surprisingly, it was her grandfather, an ex-governor, who taught her how to dance and sing. She inculcates that knowledge to her daughter and granddaughter who perform in the festival. María shares that the dances they perform are inspired by nature. For example, *La Rana* features bright clothes and skin decorations because frogs are very colorful, jump everywhere, and make murmuring sounds all the time. She makes a point to signal to her decorated arms and legs as she relays this information. Every three weeks her community gathers to dance, draw, tell stories to the children, and make colorfully intricate beaded jewelery and blouses. They encourage the children to dress in Embera culture's clothes, jewelery, and fabrics because many are losing their heritage and she wants to engage in "cultural uplift" work.

The day after the dance festival in Santa María la Antigua del Darién, the inauguration of the municipal park in Unguía took place. Omar's dance group performed an Afro-Colombian polka-waltz, while eight of the Guna Tule youth from Arquía reprised their performance from the day before. When María was asked whether she would be attending the event in Unguía the following day, she said she didn't know that "the ones from Arquía" would be dancing there. "If we get invited, we go, but we weren't invited, they invite the ones from Arquía, but not us." Is *convivencia* a way to navigate when and where one should or should not be? It does not pretend to be an easy or even fair exercise in this instance.

All the dances were performed under a large open-air thatched roof hut or *palapa*. Bystanders could stand around the periphery of the space making room in the center for the dances. Some sat on plastic patio chairs common in these modest areas of Colombia, while children and agile adults sat on the concrete floor. Occasionally, a dog would wander in and gaze at the activity curiously. It scurried away at the gentle insistence of an audience member's sibilant sounds (sss---sss---sss). During the *abozao* an

Afro-Colombian girl dancer pulsed her shoulders and torso, while a young Embera girl, seated on the ground by her, began to imitate the movements. The Afro-Colombian dances featured drumming and clapping, but there was a lack of audience participation or call-and-response. I also noticed many serious expressions watching the dances and dancers regardless of who was dancing. What if these expressions are actually a form of curious engagement? A way to experience difference despite a commonality based around shared territory?

The dances offered stark gendered contrast which heightened the cultural specificities of each community. Men wore pants, women wore skirts or dresses: flounces and ruffles adorned the Afro-Colombian ones, while bright patterns and colors played on the sarong skirts of all three Indigenous tribes. The Embera dances exclusively showcased girls and women. The Afro-Colombian dances offered equal gender participation but very gendered movements and division of labor. The *Guna Dule* featured both boys and girls dancing and playing instruments.

Choreographically, all of the dances relied on unison. Entrances and exits required each dancer to be attentive to the space in front or behind so that there would be enough room for each of them to execute their movements. It was important to watch and follow one another. Repetition of movement phrases abounded: forward weight shift hops, side skip sways, with diagonal turns and spiral like paths through the space (Guna Dule dance *La Zeta*/The Zed); quick, bounded diagonal leaps side to side with legs pressed together (Embera Cuti dance *La Rana*); side to side lateral sways of hips and shoulder shimmies (Afro-Colombian *mapalé*). Afro-Colombian dancers featured folkloric choreographic strategies of lines and diagonals, while the Embera and Guna Dule dances highlighted circular formations and the spiral that is part of their cosmology.[13] Did it matter that some dancers were out of sync with the rhythm or with one another? What if someone forgot part of the dance? How did the young Embera dancer learn to fix her falling sarong while still maintaining the downbeat and not fall out of sync with Maria's singing or her group's hunched forward steps? I wonder what those Guna Dule and Colombian mestizo appearing boys over there are going to do with the video footage they are recording on their phones. Did it matter to them if they couldn't see all the dances properly depending on where they stood? Where did the dog go? What is that journalist with the fancy camera going to do with those photos?[14] Will they put them in the museum next to the objects unearthed from Dariena? Where is that little boy running to while Guna Dule women dance?

Closing Considerations

Philosopher Franco Berardi turns to an Indigenous woman, the Aztec Malinalli (historicized as La Malinche), in order to help him make sense of the end of the world. He wonders, "what happens when a world dies, when outside flows of semiosis overpower and outperform existing languages and forms of life, and an entire world of values, expectations, and moral codes disintegrates?"[15] Berardi considers La Malinche outside of her dichotomized role as both traitor and figurative founding mother of Mexico. Instead, for him, she represents the consciousness of someone who "knows that her world as a system of consistent cultural and semiotic references has disintegrated."[16] This is an advantageous position for it allows the individual to "transform the collapse of her world into the creation of a new language, and therefore of a new world [. . .] . Only when one is able to see collapse as the obliteration of memory, identity, and as the end of a world can a new world be imagined."[17] Staging a dance festival might be one way to generate a new post-conflict world in this area. Although the particular festival's dependence on funding by state-sanctioned organizations (ICANH and Ministry of Culture involvement) affects the full autonomy of the festival (would it have taken place without the presence of ICANH?), it did not seem to affect the content of the festival itself. The communities had authority over what to represent to one another. It remains uncertain whether the wish of these communities to have three yearly festivals will come to fruition. As of the writing of this chapter, the armed conflict has escalated in the area. Perhaps this humble festival represents what Donna Haraway envisions in *Staying with the Trouble*: "new practices of imagination, resistance, revolt, repair, and mourning, and living and dying well."[18] She insists that these types of practices must be developed—through localized dance festivals in conflict zones for example—for a "common liveable world must be composed, bit by bit, or not at all."[19]

In her notes, Isabel writes that once the event concluded, some of the community members who reside in the park gathered in a hut to watch the *fútbol* match between Colombia and Argentina. In the hut facing them, the final preparations were underway for a *quinceañera*. Pink and silver balloons bobbed in the air. This is what *convivencia* looks like here. A way of existing, literally, over the remains of a lost colonial world (*Dariena*), while simultaneously constructing something new in the aftermath of destruction and displacement. This new world is one where its inhabitants, despite the afterlife of (the ongoing) violence, managed to find time to gather, if only briefly, and "enhance [their] capacity for *being with* others"[20] one summer afternoon.

Notes

1. Katerina Paramana, "The Animation of Contemporary Subjectivity in Tino Sehgal's *Ann Lee*," *Performance Research* 24, no. 6 (2019): 114–21. Quoted in: Katerina Paramana, "Performance, Dance and Political Economy: A Provocation," this volume.

2. Anita Gonzalez, "Recognizing Race and Class in Dance: Gonzalez Response to Paramana," this volume.

3. Paolo Vignolo, "Santa María de la Antigua del Darién, ¿De lugar del olvido a lugar de la memoria?" *Historia, cultura y sociedad colonial. Siglos XVI-XVIII. Temas, problemas y perspectiva*s (2008): 321–31.

4. The municipality of Unguía has 15,000 inhabitants per the census. It contains the urban center, five corregimientos (Balboa, Tanela, Santa María, Gilgal y Titumate), three Indigenous territories (resguardos) of Embera (Dogibí-Eyakera, Tanela y Cuti), one Indigenous resguardo Cuna/Kune/Gune-Tule (Arquía), and five collective territories from the councils of Afrodescended Communities of Marriaga, El Puerto, Tarena, Ticolé, and Turmaradó. This information can be found in Alcaldía Municipal de Unguía. *Plan de Desarrollo 2016-2019*, 21–7.

5. Jesús Emilio Ramírez, "Proyecto del canal interoceánico Atrato Truandó (Colombia) a nivel del mar," *Boletín de la Sociedad Geográfica de Colombia* 25 (1967): 95–6, https://www.sogeocol.edu.co/documentos/096_proy_del_can_inter.pdf.

6. Giorgio Agamben, *Means without Ends: Notes on Politics* (Minneapolis: University of Minnesota Press, 2000), 84–5.

7. Achille Mbembe, *Necropolitics* (Durham, NC: Duke Univerity Press, 2019), 27.

8. The afterlife of political violence comes from the work of Macarena Gómez-Barris.

9. There are plans to open up the area for tourism but the ongoing conflict interrupts the Ministry of Culture initiative. Local residents have been exposed to gastronomy and hospitality training to begin preparing them for the tourism boom desired by the state in that region. It is a form of state incentivization through a neoliberal tourist economy, which unfortunately extracts/exploits both the land and the people.

10. As of this writing my research team has been informed that there has been increased paramilitary presence in Unguía and many community leaders have been threatened, including Mónica. She may no longer be in

Unguía right now. Community leaders are the biggest targets right now in Colombia. Many are threatened and/or killed with impunity.

11 I have seen the name of the tribe spelled Guna, Kuna, and Cuna, Gune-Tule, and Gune Dule. These are possible ways in Latinate languages to approximate the guttural sound of their tribe's name. Anthropologist Maurizio Alí seems to have written the only book in Spanish language about the Kuna: *En estado de sitio: los kuna en Urabá. Vida cotidiana de una comunidad indígena en una zona de conflicto*. Universidad de Los Andes, Facultad de Ciencias Sociales, Departamento de Antropología. Bogota: Uniandes, 2010.

12 Macarena Gómez-Barris, *Where Memory Dwells: Culture and State Violence in Chile* (Berkeley: UC Press, 2009), 6.

13 Some of the layout of the Archaeological Park is based on the *Gune-Dule* cosmology of the spiral.

14 He was hired by the ICANH for the event.

15 Franco "Bifo" Berardi, *And: The Phenomenology of the End* (Pasadena: Semiotexte, 2015), 332.

16 Ibid., 335.

17 Ibid.

18 Donna Haraway, *Staying with the Trouble: Making Kin in the Chthulucene* (Durham: Duke University Press, 2016), 51.

19 Ibid., 40.

20 Paramana, "The Animation of Contemporary Subjectivity in Tino Sehgal's *Ann Lee*," quoted in: Paramana, "Performance, Dance and Political Economy: A Provocation," this volume.

10 CHANGING OUR BODIES' RELATION-SHIPS TO REALITY

Usva Seregina

(A Response to Videos From the Playlist)

The power structures of contemporary capitalism exist due to their steady repetition, a repetition that largely relies on the idea that our world is a fixed entity, which is impossible or, at the very least, very difficult to change. One way we can bring light to the false fixity of our everyday life is by changing our bodies' positions within those power structures. In this chapter, I discuss two performances, *Spatial Confessions* and *FORCE,* that engage in breaking the idea of reality in this manner (see Figure 2).

Spatial Confessions changes the traditional relationship between performer and spectator by allowing the audience to be a part of restructuring reality. In this performance by Bojana Cvejić and Christine de Smedt, audience members are invited into a room and are asked to respond bodily to a series of questions read out by de Smedt.[1] The questions are relatively easy, but address various socioeconomic issues one does not typically discuss or possibly even think about.[2]

In answering the questions, participants move around and gesture in space, thus creating formations in relation to their own body and to other people. Many answers require negotiation, both verbal and bodily, pushing people to face each other—both literally and metaphorically—and position themselves in relation to one another in a very direct way. The result can be described as a series of embodied graphs or bodily networks created as

FIGURE 2 *Spatial Confessions* by Bojana Cvejić and Christine De Smedt, Turbine Hall, Tate Modern, 2014. Photo by Lennart Laberenz.

a result of the expression of individual values, opinions, and characteristics through physical movement.

The performance allows for reflection and self-reflection through asking individuals to actively engage in the performance by facing and having embodied interactions with others, thus co-creating physical constellations. In facing others in everyday life, we make immediate assumptions about who they are and how their lives are set up. When having to directly relate ourselves to these strangers, as in *Spatial Confessions,* we are forced to reconsider our preconceptions of others as well as the norms on which these preconceptions are based. Such a setting allows for discovery of one's place in society, as individuals are pushed to consider their specific place among physical, spatial, and socioeconomic connections.

In such a performance, individuals are both performers and spectators, taking on a dual role in the interaction and thus also having two levels of communication among participants. This creates a context for more nuanced and complex self-reflection, as one has to juggle two levels of representation and interaction in the setting that they are engaging. The duality allows for a performance that is distinctly *non-naturalized*, that is, one that is not being blindly repeated based on a history and normative structure of social rules of conduct. In other worlds, non-naturalized performance does not follow norms or blueprints unlike most everyday interaction, which becomes normalized through socialization and repetition. As a result of the duality of performance, the performer slowly becomes aware of *how* they are performing, leading to reflection on how they repeat norms that constitute reality, how they have been acculturated into these norms, and how they retain a role in the repetition of structures of reality.[3]

Christian Falsnaes's *FORCE* takes the dynamic of audience participation into a somewhat different direction.[4] In this performance, there is no artist present. The audience rather faces an empty stage and several sets of headphones. Spectators become performers by putting on headphones, walking onto the stage, and following prerecorded commands that they receive into their earpieces.[5] The commands are seemingly simple, but surprisingly difficult, as many include elements commonly thought to be out of place in public space. Performer-spectators are pushed to interact with the space, with their own bodies, and with other individuals in the space. They walk, dance, lay down, shout, sing, get undressed, and touch themselves all over their body. The result is an almost painful and distinct awareness of one's body in the space and in relation to other bodies.

In engaging with this performance at the Museum of Modern Art Kiasma (Helsinki, Finland), I found myself questioning my every movement and decision. Having put on the headphones, I found the orders quite easy to follow at first: I was to walk in particular parts of the stage and stand in certain positions. Three others were on stage with me; a total of four headphones were available. Other performers were moving around the space in different ways, clearly following different sets of directions. One person danced and sang; another rolled around on the floor; the third ran around in circles. I became very aware of what they were doing in addition to what I was doing so we would not collide.

I was next asked to shout certain words. I did, but immediately realized I was speaking rather than shouting. I became extremely self-aware that shouting is not something that is normally done at an art museum or in any public space. I wondered why it was so difficult for me to raise my voice: was I embarrassed? Was it because I did not want to draw attention to myself or break some sort of norm? Or was it because I have been taught to be quiet and not make a fuss?

With my brain filled with questions, I could not find any logical answer for why not to shout and hence found it easier to start shouting at the top of my lungs. This immediately drew the attention of more and more people. Quite a large crowd started to gather around the stage, which made me feel even more self-aware. As we were in a large museum, I could not help but wonder, do these people know what type of performance they are observing? Are they aware that I am not the artist behind this piece? Or have I become one of the artists now?

Toward the end of my performance, I was given instructions to take off items that I might have been wearing. First a bag, then a jacket, shoes, a hat. Then I was asked to take off a shirt, pants, a dress, a skirt, underwear, until the listener should, in theory, be absolutely naked. I must admit I did not take all of my clothes off. At the end of the recording that was giving me directions, I was still wearing pants and a sports bra.

The process of taking off my clothing slowly bit by bit in public as a result of instructions only I could hear was a rather intriguing experience, during which I put a great deal of thought to every decision I made. For upper layers of clothing, I had absolutely no trouble taking things off as instructed. However, as the recording began to get to layers one does not normally take off in public, I began to be more and more self-aware. I am not a person who is ashamed of nudity, but I began to question how other people in the space would feel, as they may not be aware of the work's potential inclusion of nudity. Would they feel uncomfortable? Angered? As the space is a large museum, individuals kept walking past, not fully knowledgeable of the nature of the performance on stage. I began to fear unwanted glances on my body that I was slowly unveiling, even potential unwanted photography. All attention was on me at this point, because those who I had shared the stage with had started earlier and thus their recordings had already ended.

As I began to disobey the orders I was hearing through the headphones, the strongest emotion I felt was shame. And not shame for my body, but shame for not following the instructions. Was I engaging in the performance incorrectly? Will others be disappointed? In questioning my own disobedience, I began to realize the importance of pushing back against authority and normative structures that make one feel uncomfortable. Moreover, I pushed back on the authority of the artist, making the performance my own in many ways. I exited the performance with a strong feeling of ownership over my own body and my own boundaries, having so clearly decided how far my own limits of comfort can be pushed.

While people react to this performance in different ways, overall, from my perspective, the experience results in awareness of one's body in space and in relation to others. This raises questions about how one normally acts, interacts, and positions one's body in relation to others and in relation to public space. Suddenly, norms feel strange and almost silly, with their power dwindling over our lives.

To reflect on the two performances, both *Spatial Confessions* and *FORCE* aim at disrupting existing normative structures by deconstructing the familiar relationship of one's body to space and to others. This is done in order to reshuffle the convenient social structures of our everyday lives in ways that makes us feel unsettled. The unease makes one reflect not only on the performance at hand, but also on the normative structures that it ruptures by making them visible and questioning them.

In *Spatial Confessions*, the spectators become a part of the performance, thus having to literally place their bodies into new relationships with others. The artist in this context becomes a sort of authority, as they are physically present and giving direct orders. Moreover, other participants/performers provide a sense of panopticon: all actions are being observed and judged by others. This influences engagement with the performance in several ways. On the one hand, one gains recognition and legitimization for their actions from others. On the other hand, if one has "unpopular" or "controversial" responses to the questions asked, these may be difficult to enact, which could result in extreme discomfort for the individual or "untruthful" outcomes for the performance overall. In any case, the presence of others as well as of an authoritative figure clearly forces one to reconsider one's own position in relation to others through a variety of socioeconomic characteristics, resulting in a self-awareness and self-questioning that is fertile ground for learning.

In *FORCE*, the participant is, in many ways, left alone, which can have both positive and negative repercussions that are largely contingent on the character of those performing. The spectator-performer is not subject to any direct authority; unlike *Spatial Confessions*, the artist who guides the performance is not present and the other performers do not respond to the same instructions. Ultimately, the spectator-performer is given responsibility for the performance, their own body, and the way they place that body onstage, as it is up to them to decide whether or not they will obey and, if they do, how they will enact that order. If the spectator-performer does nothing or does something differently, no one will know (as only they can hear the recording), and hence it becomes a quandary for their conscience to mull over. The audience that is not interacting with the recordings may, however, become a monitoring presence, causing the spectator-performer to alter how they behave and respond to the instructions heard through the headphones. The overall result is an exploration of personal boundaries and one's individual relationship to normative power structures.

These types of performances are examples of ways I believe dance can engage in critiquing the political economy, thus entering a conversation about its future development. Such performances push the spectators to become a part of the art-making by requiring bodily engagement and asking open-ended questions to ponder and critique, rather than by providing direct answers. Through having to make a leap of faith into the unknown and create their own meaning, individuals begin to analyze and interpret for themselves, uncovering the norms, structures, and roles by which their lives are governed.[6]

As with any proposition, several issues emerge. First, such performances are very demanding of their spectators, as individuals have to become a part of them and to engage in them critically. This raises the question of who the ideal target audience is, and, more importantly, who the audience is in practice. As noted in other chapters in this book, class plays a huge role in how individuals are exposed to art and the tools needed to engage with it. Because the type of performance described here requires active participation, it also requires a certain acculturation to be able to interact with it. We cannot force individuals to be interested or emotionally and physically committed, and if they do not have the cultural capital needed to engage, they could potentially be left out.

Another issue is the potential lack of meaning in the work or extremely abstracted meaning derived by spectators, as these performances are of an open-ended nature. In deconstructing or pushing others to deconstruct meaning, performances as the ones described above end up presenting no direct solutions of their own. This can potentially lead to meaning that is far removed from social and political concerns of everyday life. Auslander fears that this may result in individuals exploring only their own inner worlds, thus disregarding the context they reside in. Such an approach is helpful in alleviating personal confusion, but not very applicable to large-scale, communal issues of everyday life.[7]

To address both issues, I believe performances such as those described earlier could push for even further contextualization. Both performances already do a great job in getting people to participate physically, mentally, and emotionally with their context. Moreover, in developing the performances, the artists directly engaged with the context of their work. For instance, Cvejić and de Smedt asked participants about their socioeconomic status and living quarters before accepting them to be a part of the performance. Such an approach allowed for more diverse emergent meanings and interactions, as participants were pushed to face those who are outside their normal social circles. However, to engage a variety of socioeconomic groups as well as to help those who are most vulnerable, I believe it is important to directly interact with contexts that do not readily engage in artistic performances (be it due to lack of time, money, or even because of social stigma or acculturation). In working with communities and in communities by engaging individuals in dance performance that they would not normally be exposed to, we allow them access to knowledge and understanding that is different from what they are used to. As can be seen in both of the described performances, working within communities results in building meaning together and contextually, which allows for addressing structures with and for those who they specifically have power over.

We have the potential to rediscover our bodies and reconfigure their places in our realities. To accomplish this, we need to make ourselves uncomfortable and to question our realities by performing in ways we did not know we could. This means encountering topics we normally do not, engaging in interactions we normally do not have, and performing bodily movements in ways we normally do not. Through dance, we are pushed to engage our world in ways that break normalized structures of our daily lives and look at them with a fresh pair of eyes. By interrupting the flow of normalized reality, we are able to think of and begin to create a better future.

Notes

1 Bojana Cvejić and Christine de Smedt, *Spatial Confessions* (London, UK: Tate Modern, 2014). https:// www.youtube.com/watch?v=_PEDcLVVUdc

2 Examples of questions:

"Arrange yourself in a line according to the color of your skin."
"If you share your living space with other people, take a step forward."
"If you own your living space, turn around."
"If you think London is overcrowded, go stand behind someone else."
"If you are unsure of what public space is and who owns it, come together in a tight group in the left corner."

3 Anastasia Seregina, *Performing Fantasy and Reality in Contemporary Culture* (London: Routledge, 2019); see also Bertold Brecht, *Театр: Пьесы. Статьи. Высказывания* (Isskusstvo: Moscow, 1965).

4 Christian Falsnaes, *FORCE* (2018). https://youtu.be/n-lwoBlGdkY

5 Examples of instructions: "Put both of your hands on another person; move your hands from head to foot. Jump forward as far as you can. Start moving your hands over your entire body and touch every part of yourself."

6 Brecht, *Театр: Пьесы. Статьи. Высказывания*; Vsevolod E. Meyerhold, *Статьи, письма, речи, беседы* (Isskusstvo: Moscow, 1968).

7 Philip Auslander, *Presence and Resistance: Postmodernism and Cultural Politics in Contemporary American Performance* (Ann Arbor: The University of Michigan Press, 1992).

DIALOGUE 5
ANARCHIC INVERSIONS OF NEOLIBERAL ECONOMIES

Melissa Blanco Borelli's "The 'End,' 'Lived Time' or How to Say Goodbye to Your World, A World" is a performative text about endings and the "end of the world" based on her reading of four performances. Elena Loizidou's "Dance, Anarchism, Mutual Aid" examines the affinities between dance and anarchism, insights they offer into one another, and ways they can aid constructing a new politico-economic model. Dialogue 5 proposes different strategies for combating and ending the current global political economy both through anarchist thinking and through the prism of performance.

11 THE "END," "LIVED TIME" OR HOW TO SAY GOODBYE TO YOUR WORLD, A WORLD

Melissa Blanco Borelli

(A Response to Videos from the Playlist)

Sometimes thinking about the end of the world can be exciting. Besides offering some *jouissance* to those of us who enjoy a bit of gallows humor, it offers an opportunity to imagine an elsewhere somewhere after the end. The idea of "the end" promises a totalizing moment, one that stubbornly stops and forbids the forcefulness of time to barrel on. It signals an end of time, or within the neoliberal capitalist context, an inability to fulfill its demands for productivity and resource accumulation. An end can also bring us to question our current political economic system that stunts our time for reflection and imagination, and makes many of us long for its end. The possibility to imagine what happens after, if there even *is* an after, after the "end," appears in different ways in the context of these four works I am grouping together under this open-ended idea of "the end." These pieces, in their capacious imagining of "ends," allow dance to become a prism for politics, specifically echoing Mark Franko's claim that "[p]olitics are not located directly 'in' dance, but in the way dance manages to occupy (cultural) space."[1] It is for this reason that dance is "ideological, and . . . carries inevitable political effects."[2] As such, these different choreographed iterations present ways that dance imagines other political modes of being in the world after an "end."

- Work 1: The end of a parent's life as the genesis of a new relationship to one's own mortality. (Becky Edmunds's *Goodbye, Love*)
- Work 2: The familiar world of home, family, and friends becoming a nostalgic desire or distant memory after immigration or exile. (The Blaze's music video for "Territory")
- Work 3: Flipping one's visible and situated perspective of the world and thinking-feeling alongside plant and animal. (nibia pastrano santiago's *danza actual o el evento coreográfico*)
- Work 4: And lastly, a desperate, gluttonous act after the "end of the world" to make do. What happens when everything is at its end? (Wangechi Mutu + Santigold, *The End of Eating Everything*)[3]

These four artistic works not only offer a proposition about an end but attempt to answer what art theorist Natalie Loveless wonders when she asks, "How might we *inhabit* human, nonhuman, never-been-human, and more-than-human social webs differently at all scales of existence?"[4] If an end or *the* end is inevitable, what creative and imaginative modes can we enlist to turn these endings into something else? How do you continue to exist *after* an end? What world(s) rise up that offer new ways of being? How does an end signal an inevitable beginning? Continuation in the same way after an end is no longer viable. So, how to end-ure?

Becky Edmunds's *Goodbye, Love*

Losing a parent signals an end of a world. A world to which one is tethered through a genealogical connection to another person, two people, who made a decision to bring you into their world, and the world, and help you see it and perhaps make it better. Becky Edmunds's *Goodbye, Love* poignantly depicts the feelings of love and loss in less than three minutes. In the video we see Super-8 film footage of a man full of vitality and humor. He offers his hand to the toddler in the footage as he lies on his deathbed; and it is presumably his hand that to which the narrator refers via the film's superimposed text. This simple gesture of holding a loved one's hand at the end of their life appeases the inevitability of mortality. In that gesture, which we never see but can imagine each time the text repeats "on Friday I held your hand," I find myself wondering about the end of gestural reciprocity. She will hold his hand, but hers will never be held by his again. Yet performance studies scholar Rebecca Schneider's claim about gesture opens up another possibility. She writes, "a gesture, like a wave, is at once an act in and capable of reiteration, but also an action extended, opening the possibility of future alteration."[5] It is this idea of future alteration where I want to pause for a moment. Might we imagine the changes in the gesture as moving from material embodied exchange to something else, something surreal, something otherworldly beyond the dull mortality of the human flesh? The capacious potential that "an end" offers beyond death only makes the gesture more meaningful. Death here is not an end, but a moment to reflect on life, connection, and the poetry of existence.

The Blaze, Music Video for "Territory"

Leaving your native country signals an end of a world. The familiar can no longer be felt, touched, sensed, smelled, experienced. New sounds lull and disturb. If lucky, they might also drown out the pain of nostalgia and longing for home. The young Algerian men dancing, smoking, running, and crying in The Blaze's video for their song "Territory" show what home means for them. The video functions as a documentary of migrant longings for home, longings that leave imprints like the wake of the ship in the Mediterranean at the start of the video.

Besides being an actual space of dwelling, home exists as a feeling of camaraderie. Shadow-boxing in the dark with your friends, while the diegetic soundtrack punctuates every jab or thrust. Dancing ecstatically on the roof with those same friends, enjoying the bird's eye view of your hometown, homeland. The long, drawn out embrace of farewell in someone's arms. Their hands on your cheek stopping the inevitable trail of tears. The crowded comfort of sleeping with everyone in the same beds. These moments of private and public Algerian masculinity provide glimpses of how an end of a domestic world changes the time in which we experience or even remember that world. The video relies on slow motion action shots, especially during the significant dance scene on the roof, to articulate the residue of memory and time before this end of the world. In this sense, this time before "the end" does not necessarily fall into temporal linearity. Instead, the Algerian men enact what philosopher Henri Bergson considers as "lived time," time made up of lived experience, affect, and embodiment.[6] Bergson proposes fantasy, hoping, and dreaming as ways to create a future, an after the end in the case of "Territory." So while these men look back (as is suggested by the video and its use of slow motion) in order to endure the look forward/toward (a) (their) new world as migrants across the Mediterranean, time no longer exists. The comforting mise-en-scéne of "lived time" supplants it. He barrels across the roof, leaning forward while shaking his head vigorously, tongue wagging out of his mouth. His torso leans forward, his arms curve inwards, and he makes circular motions with his arms while he rotates his torso. He spins around joyously. The cigarette in his hand and later in his mouth is just another red light in the scene. It keeps company with the red lights fired up in the town below as dusk settles into night. All the while, he dances, filmed in slow motion, arms reaching toward the sky, his face with a look of ecstasy. In that moment, he lives. His end is not before or after this time. His end, his before, and his after are all there with him on his roof in his territory. There can be no end when everything feels joyful in the present.

nibia pastrana santiago, *danza actual o el evento coreográfico: estructuras temporales para provocar un evento imposible*

nibia pastrana santiago's world creeps on; it has not ended at all. Yet, she slowly and meticulously considers a new one. A new quotidian reality that begins from merely shifting her perspective. Sometimes she physically experiences it upside down. In other instances, she incorporates the plant or the dog in the space as part of her choreography of an everyday (see Figures 3 and 4). In an act of interspecies solidarity, she purposely resists turning the plant and the dog into props. Instead, pastrana santiago thinks about her own world from their perspective. She lays on the floor in front of her (a) dog and acknowledges it. She communicates with it. She vocalizes to it. She whimpers and growls in different registers. In another instance when the dog is sitting with audience members in the domestic living room space where this performance takes place, pastrana santiago sits next to

FIGURES 3 AND 4 nibia pastrana santiago, Tara (Golden Retriever) and seagrape, *danza actual o el evento coreográfico: estructuras temporales para provocar un evento imposible (Current dance or the choreographic event: temporary structures to provoke an impossible event)*, 2015, Casa del Sargento Beta-Local, San Juan, Puerto Rico. Photo: Tony Cruz.

the dog, leans lovingly against it, and begins to "become dog." She pants and sticks out her tongue. Another audience member (Puerto Rican dance scholar Susan Homar) strokes her back as she makes these gestures. The strokes resemble the ones pastrana santiago gave the dog earlier. In this undoing of a quotidian human world, pastrana santiago offers her viewers the possibility to think about how a new interspecies world might be; one where human, plant, and animal coexist.

On the wall, we are privy to her choreographic ideas and propositions. They read as directions, ideas, or even movement scores:

Acompañar la planta	Accompany the plant
Activar lo salvaje	Activate the savage
Si aparece un gato: reconocerlo	If a cat appears: acknowledge it
Desplazamiento en 2 patas, 4 patas	Displacement on 2 legs, 4 legs
Afecto humano	Human affect
Devenir perra	Become bitch (female dog)
Devenir planta	Become plant
Emoción canina	Canine emotion

Human emotion is on the same level of importance as canine one. Becoming plant or becoming (a female) dog are important. This seems like a dance piece feminist philosopher Donna Haraway might appreciate. She wrote several stories about her relationship with her dog. *The Companion Species Manifesto* (2003) and *When Species Meet* (2007) consider Haraway's own sense of identity and meaning in relation to touching her dog. She asks, "How is 'becoming with' a practice of becoming worldly?"[7] This consistent "becoming with" that Haraway proposes affects our every day, it constitutes the worlds in which we live. pastrana santiago's staging of time in *danza actual o el evento coreográfico: estructuras temporales para provocar un evento imposible* (2015) materializes what Latina/o studies scholar Sandra Ruiz labels as Ricanness; that is, a continual performance of bodily endurance against US colonialism through a different measure of time.[8] In the event's impossibility, as the title states, lies its infinite possibility. pastrana santiago's provocation can only happen through her relationship with *la planta* and *la perra*. Impossibility here relies on the power to create a different mode of enduring colonial time only further stultified after the end of Hurricane Maria. After so much destruction, what can a body do but endure? This search of an impossible event, through durational choreography as a way to think about the violence of time and its never-end-ingness . . . . This. This is an end unto itself.

Wangechi Mutu + Santigold, *The End of Eating Everything*

When the end of the world is finally over, she looks ahead . . . for a signal . . . for some prey.

> *Birds flying high, you know how I feel . . .*[9]

I wonder if that song lies muffled in the remains of black arms, legs, blood, wheels, viscera, toxic waste, and hair that inches forward. She continues to search with loving regard. She smells. Her tensile hair breathes for her. What can it breathe in that atmosphere? It expands and contracts and mirrors her emotions . . . when she shows them. Oh, she will show them. She looks down at the black birds. She curls her lip upward. Her nostrils react to the smell. They rise up and flare ever so slightly.

> *Can I eat them?* Her face seems to query. She is hungry.
> *We've always been hungry, alone and together.*[10]

She speaks to her body full of others like her. Bioluminescent remains of once skeletal bodies offer the only color and light in that atmosphere. Never forget that bioluminescence comes from the calcium and magnesium in the stars which are in our bones. When it shimmers on the sea, we remember those bones below.

With one forceful inhalation, in-hair-ation, breath and body come together and let out a scream. A scream of finality. An announcement. A pronouncement. With that she begins to devour the birds. Blood appears like mist. She continues. Ravenous. Greedy. Gluttonous. Her engorged body appears bigger, brighter, shinier. It glistens with . . . Is that vitality? What does it mean to be alive after such a catastrophic calamity? What does it mean to be Black and alive after such a catastrophic calamity? The detritus of the Middle Passage clings to her and along with that the waste leftover after the end of the world. Yet, she continues. After she finishes her meal, she continues. She plods forward until she disappears (or dissipates) behind thick grey clouds.

> After annihilation and destruction, she remains.
> After breathing and eating, she remains.
> She remains after the "end."

In the end, an end of something is not an end to everything. Instead, endings in these four works demonstrate how mortality, immigration, the end of a perspective, and survival after an apocalypse can signal ways in which dance and performance practices can provide examples on how to reshape the world. Old politics must die in order for progressive ones to enter the political sphere. Changing spaces and places of home helps us encounter one another differently and hopefully with more compassion. Shifting our perspectives physically and metaphorically invites new possibilities for creation and, lastly, the presence of an appetite (desire or even will) to keep on going and existing signals some hope for us despite the many ends we must endure.

Notes

1 Mark Franko, "Dance and the Political: States of Exception," *Dance Research Journal* 38, no. 1/2 (Summer–Winter 2006), 3–18, p. 5.

2 Ibid., 6.

3 Becky Edmunds, *Goodbye, Love* (2015): https://vimeo.com/151298203; The Blaze, "Territory" (2017): https://www.youtube.com/watch?v=54fea7wuV6s; nibia pastrano santiago, *danza actual o el evento coreográfico* (2015): https://vimeo.com/154271141; Wangechi Mutu + Santigold, *The End of Eating Everything* (2013): https://youtube.com/watch?v=wMZSCfqOxVs.

4 Natalie Loveless, *How to Make Art at the End of the World* (Durham: Duke University Press, 2018), 100.

5 Rebecca Schneider, "That the Past May Yet Have Another Future: The History of Gesture in the Time of Hands Up," *Theatre Journal* 70, no. 3 (September 2018): 285–306, p. 286.

6 Henri Bergson, *Time and Free Will: An Essay on the Immediate Data of Consciousness* (Mineola, NY: Dover, 2001), 100.

7 Donna Haraway, *When Species Meet* (Minneapolis: University of Minnesota Press, 2007), 3.

8 Sandra Ruiz, *Ricanness: Enduring Time in Anticolonial Performance* (New York: New York University Press, 2018).

9 Lyrics from Nina Simone's "Feeling Good," lyrics by Anthony Newley and Leslie Bricusse, Universal Music Publishing, 1965.

10 Text from the video.

12 DANCE, ANARCHISM, MUTUAL AID

Elena Loizidou

(A Response to the Editors' Provocations)

Prelude

What do dance and anarchism have in common? Although some commonalities between them will be undoubtedly identified, what I am more interested in here is seeing what kind of world emerges when an anarchist such as Emma Goldman utters the words "anarchism" and "dance" together. I follow the philosopher Giorgio Agamben's definition of dance as explored in his essay "Notes on Gesture."[1] Dance, he writes, is a gesture that communicates *movement* and *support*.[2] Importantly, dance communicates a type of politics that has movement and support at its core. The type of politics that dance gestures toward (defined as pure politics or pure means by Agamben[3]) is the *opposite* of neoliberal politics (securitization, fixity, profit, competition[4]). Agamben's understanding of dance, I suggest, coincides with the politics of mutual support, antiauthoritarianism, and movement that anarchism propagates.

In Part One of the chapter, I discuss how Emma Goldman uses dance to explain what anarchism is for her (beyond the definition of anarchism as antiauthoritarian and so forth, as I have already indicated) and simultaneously critiques any type of politics that persists in separating the various areas of life (political, social, ethical, aesthetic). In Part Two of the chapter, I unpick *how* anarchism offers a different art of living based on mutual aid or support—the second element I have suggested dance communicates. Indeed, literally speaking, dancers bolster each other in their performances. I explain how Kropotkin's theory of mutual aid explores a way of organizing life that is *neither* based on hierarchies *nor* competition, *nor* restricts movements or celebrates securitization, all characteristics of our neoliberal times and economies.

Part One: Dance and Anarchism

Emma Goldman was a well-known, US-based anarchist activist, writer, and orator. She was born in Kovno of the Russian Empire in 1869 to a Jewish family. On December 29, 1885, she along with her sister Helena got on a boat from Russia to meet their other sister Lena and her husband in Rochester, New York, USA. Four years later, on August 8, 1889, Goldman left Rochester and her husband Jacob Kershner, whom she had married in 1886, and moved to New York City to serve the anarchist cause. Her decision to serve the anarchist cause stemmed from a deep sense of injustice she felt when she heard of the execution of the seven Haymarket anarchists in Chicago. They were executed after they were found guilty of killing a police officer during a peaceful demonstration which demanded the introduction of the eight-hour workday. Goldman was not a blind ideologue. She may had been an anarchist, holding onto a particular political ideology, but she was also able to acknowledge anarchism's shortcomings, for instance, when the ideology was unable to represent what was going on in life or whenever it came close to bolstering conventions. For example, when Goldman went on a lecture tour after John Most, a well-known German anarchist, he convinced her that she will be helping the anarchist cause. Goldman found herself unhappy with ventriloquizing his speeches, which omitted any discussion of the eight-hour workday struggle—the burning issue for every worker in the United States at the time. Goldman critiqued and confronted Most and abandoned his project. She experienced Most's anarchist project as empty and distant from the realities that plagued the working class in the United States. Anarchism for her was not just an ideal but a sociopolitical philosophy that reflected and emanated from the everyday concerns of the people. If anarchism was an ideology that propagated the loss of authority (neither rule nor ruler) then its very actions or struggles, Goldman believed, should be embracing and supporting the voices of the working people. For this reason, when Joseph Barondess invited her to help him organize young Jewish anarchists and socialist clockworkers to strike over this issue, she threw herself to the task and even persuaded women workers to strike. The struggle for the improvement of working conditions was for her a struggle that reflected the ethos of anarchist ideology.

It is during this period that we find Goldman also acknowledging the danger of anarchists holding conventional views and the importance of dance in revolutionary politics. During a dance organized by Joseph Barondess and other strikers, Goldman danced with vigor and enthusiasm. Her enthusiasm for dancing was not, however, appreciated by all:

> At the dances I was one of the most untiring and gayest. One evening ... a young boy, took me aside. With a grave face, as if he were about to announce the death of a dear comrade, he whispered to me that it did not behoove an agitator to dance. Certainly not with such reckless abandon, anyway. It was undignified for one who was on the way to become a force in the anarchist movement. My frivolity would only hurt the Cause. I grew furious at the impudent interference of the boy. I told him to mind his own business, I was tired of having the Cause constantly thrown into my face. I did not believe that a Cause which stood for a beautiful ideal, for anarchism, for release and freedom from conventions and prejudice, should demand the denial of life and joy. I insisted that our Cause could not expect me to become a nun and that the movement should not be turned into a cloister. If it meant that, I did not want it. "I want freedom, the right to self-expression, everybody's right to beautiful, radiant things." Anarchism meant that to me, and I would live it in spite of the whole world—prisons, persecution, everything. Yes, even in spite of the condemnation of my own closest comrades I would live my beautiful ideal.[5]

Goldman's response to the reprimands of the young anarchist may not have the punch of the slogan "If I can't dance, I don't want to be part of your revolution" that is attributed to her, but it certainly provides us with her understanding of anarchism. Dance, as you can see, becomes the instance, the *art* which she uses to provide us with a lesson *about* anarchism. Anarchism is for her more than an ideality; it is an *art* of living. And it can be truly revolutionary when it enables individuals to free themselves from "conventions and prejudices" and does not "demand the denial of life and joy."[6] We find these points explained further in her essay "Anarchism: What It Really Stands For."[7] Anarchism, she writes, is "[t]he philosophy of a new social order based on liberty unrestricted by man-made law."[8] So any conventional thinking that restricts people from doing what they need to reach their freedom is working against anarchism and, to this extent, life per se. She uses the example of the economy to explain that every solution or transformation of economic concerns should always take into account how it affects or restricts the freedom to live: "the solution of that evil can be brought about only through the consideration of *every phase* of life—individual, as well as the collective; the internal, as well as the external phases."[9] For Goldman, anarchism does not only aim to achieve economic equality for all and ameliorate dire working conditions; it also demands the transformation of all spheres of life, freeing them from "conventions and prejudice."[10] Although dance, as Agamben suggests, communicates movement and support, conventions, like rights, or any legal instruments, do not communicate movement. Conventions are instead blueprints that command us to live our lives abstractly (disembodied) and lay claim to universality, failing to adhere to our uniqueness. Even when conventions get revised to include previously excluded subjects (women, People of Color, LGBT+), they retain their structure and frame. Revised conventions still clamor *command* as their ultimate characteristic. They do not, we may say, change their mode of operation from one of *command* to one of *support* or *mutual aid*. Therefore, if dance communicates the importance of movement as Agamben suggests, then it also suggests that our lives cannot be commanded nor fixed. It is not a coincidence therefore that Goldman was prompted to talk about anarchism when she was reprimanded for dancing with frenzy. Dance, like anarchism, brings to the fore the impossibility of separating or bordering our different areas of life and reveals that any attempt to stop or hinder movement goes against the very essence of life which communicates fluidity and freedom to act in nonconventional ways. In articulating that life is movement, both anarchism and dance offer a critique to any political and socioeconomic regime such as neoliberalism, which has the economic sphere dominating over our lives and consequently takes away from us the freedom to live life in its totality. Put differently, a different politics cannot come into being if we keep separating the different spheres of life.

Similarly, Katerina Paramana[11] informs us that the separation of the study of economics from politics as well as the dominance of economics can be traced back to the 1890s and to the writings of Alfred Marshall. Indeed, as we have seen, this very critique is part and parcel of anarchism. We witness Goldman not being able to imagine that we can have a world that is economically equal while at the same time, for example, it is considered inappropriate for women to dance. For Goldman, restrictions in life due to prejudice or convention cannot deliver freedom even if there is economic prosperity.

Goldman is writing at a time when women were not fully emancipated and were considered instead property of men. Moreover, certain activities such as dance were considered to be unbecoming for women and, as we see from the reprimand she received from the young male anarchist, unacceptable for women activists. But dance as she says is joy and pleasure, and joy and pleasure are fundamental parts of our lives; we should all therefore have access to them. Through dance, she writes, she experiences a sense of freedom precisely because it caters to pleasure and joy, both necessary for a whole and good life.

Goldman's reference to dance, or rather being asked not to dance, is of course not about dance in a professional sense—that is, dance taught in studios and dance schools and performed in dance theaters and festival halls. Nevertheless, her reference to dance reminds us that in an anarchist new order, or any organization of life, we should all have access to dance or movement. Why? First, movement, the *essence* of dance, is a reminder that the various forms of life (political, economic, aesthetic, ethical) are interconnected and any politics that attempts to separate them or have economy *determining* the others, is a totalizing politics, or a politics that curbs our freedom to be anything but subjects that are subjugated to the economic. Second, as long as dance and movement exist, even under neoliberal circumstances, we will be able to see the possibility of a politics like anarchism that puts movement at its core. Without dance or access to dance, our sense of freedom, the freedom to imagine different and undifferentiated spheres of life, may be restricted.

Anita Gonzalez writes that, "[p]olitical economies affect all aspects of the dancer's life: training, aesthetics, employment, apparel, transit, and ultimately opportunity"[12] and proceeds to demonstrate how class may restrict the access that dancers have to performances and work opportunities. Gonzalez's observations, emanating from her experience as a dance scholar and practitioner, may at first glance appear to be suggesting the opposite to what Goldman was saying, because Goldman may be appearing to only be interested in the social and not also economic transformation that anarchism can bring to society. Nevertheless, Goldman would have never anticipated an anarchist new order without the amelioration of economic inequality. The inequalities that Gonzalez describes, and which plight dance, as well as our freedom of movement, cannot be ameliorated by economic changes such as a reduced taxation. They instead require a complete transformation, a revolutionary transformation of the social, economic, and political order. We don't just need dance scholarships for dancers coming from lower economic backgrounds; we need to abolish poverty and undo all prejudices that may plague dance (such as the notion that dance is unproductive for society). Dance *communicates* the type of politics that we need in order to live a joyful and pleasurable life, a life not curbed by conventions. Anarchism, through support and mutual aid as we will read later, *provides* us with such a pathway.

Part Two: Mutual Aid

Peter Kropotkin's economic and social reconceptualization of our polities, organized around the principle of mutual aid, provides us with the prospect of a world where access to pleasure and work will not be commanded by profit, prejudice, and tradition, but rather made possible by mutual aid, the abolition of private property, the distribution of wealth of all according to their needs, and space for leisure or luxury time. We have seen earlier how dance as movement articulates these as being central to living. Let's see how anarchism provides us with this pathway.

Kropotkin develops his anarcho-communist concept of mutual aid in numerous writings including *Mutual Aid*,[13] first published in 1902, and *The Conquest of Bread*,[14] first published in 1892. I will first turn to his book *Mutual Aid*. For Kropotkin, mutual aid underpins his call for anarcho-communist polity. In this book, he records the widespread instances of mutual aid within the animal and human kingdom. Kropotkin points out that Darwin, in *The Descent of Man*, talks also about how the cooperation instinct—present in animals and humans—plays a pivotal role for our survival. Darwin discovered that the instinct of cooperation or mutual aid overrides that of competition.[15] As Kropotkin avails, Darwin's followers, for their own interests, decided to focus instead on the narrow interpretation of Darwin's theory of evolution and bracketed out references to mutual support.[16] In *Mutual Aid*, Kropotkin therefore sets out to restore mutual aid to its pivotal position as a contributor to our survival, explaining how mutual aid is present within family structures (animal/human) and nonfamily-based associations. Even predatory animals, like the Brazilian Kites, he writes, practice mutual aid by sharing food and are supportive to different species like the percnopters.[17]

Moreover, Kropotkin tracks the practice of mutual aid in humans in villages and farming associations, entertainment clubs, unions, and guilds.[18] In human societies, he observes, there is an undoubtedly strong tendency toward mutual support especially when people are striving to bring about transformations in their living, working, economic, and social conditions. Mutual aid is, if we follow Kropotkin, a very established way of doing things in our world. Capitalism and neoliberal mentalities have valorized competition or the survival of the fittest, but this does not mean, and this is Kropotkin's valuable contribution, that this is the only way of doing things. Saidiya Hartman also found mutual aid practices among Black women in the United States at the beginning of the twentieth century, reminding us that mutual aid is much more widespread than we imagine it to be.[19]

Still, we may ask, did Kropotkin have a vision of how mutual aid can enable us to form polities? Did he have any suggestions as to how to transform our living worlds into ones whereby mutual aid, not capitalism, not legalism, nor the state are the dominant ways of organizing life? In *The Conquest of Bread*[20] he tracks this possibility. Peter Marshall in fact explains that Kropotkin was confident that the dispossessed would destroy the state and reestablish a way of life that will be guided by mutual aid.[21] At the place of the state he imagines the creation of voluntary associations. *The Conquest of Bread* offers multiple examples of voluntary associations— from housing to work associations—that bring together consumers and producers. These associations are envisaged having various sizes—small, big, international, and local—and being governed by free agreement. As Marshal puts it:

> It meant politically a society without government, that is anarchy, and economically, the complete negation of the wage system and the ownership of the means of production in common: "everybody, contributing for the common well-being to the full extent of his capacities, shall enjoy from the common stock of society to the fullest possible extent of his needs."[22]

As the quote reveals, Kropotkin thought that an anarcho-communist society, a mutual aid society, requires first of all the abolition of private property. The abolition of private property will come about when the dispossessed, factory workers, farmers, artisans, artists, and so on *rise* against capitalism. This will happen inevitably as capitalism will make the living of these groups impossible. We can imagine dancers who do not come from privileged economic backgrounds—Gonzalez brought to our attention such a class of dancers—becoming part of such a revolution. Kropotkin expects that when the revolution succeeds, from the "first day of the revolution the worker shall know . . . that henceforward none need crouch under the bridges, while palaces are hard by . . . none need perish with cold near shops full of furs."[23] The revolution thus will consider first the needs of people "before schooling them in their duties."[24] And in making sure that this will happen, possession of every private property will be turned into common property. After this happens, according to Kropotkin, there will be no need to establish a better wage system—where workers will be paid more fairly and in accordance to the hours they work. Such a collectivist system (that Marx followed) is untenable.[25] Why is it untenable? Because it discards that in an anarcho-communist society, where property and "the instruments of labour [are considered] common inheritance"[26] there will be no need for a wage system:

> The wage system arises out of the individual ownership of the land and the instruments of labour. It was the necessary condition for the development of capitalist production, and will perish with it, in spite of the attempt to disguise it as "profit sharing." The common possession of the instruments of labour must necessarily bring with it the enjoyment in common of the fruits of common labour.[27]

It so ensues that the abolition of a wage system and the remuneration of all according to their needs alone are the two anchors of Kropotkin's anarcho-communist society. For him such a society is possible as we witness, even in capitalist societies, mutual aid practices. He uses multiple examples to demonstrate that the capitalist society of the nineteenth century was moving toward anarcho-communism. One of his more successful examples where he identifies a communistic attitude with capitalist societies is the example of the British National Boat Institute. Kropotkin writes excitingly about this Institute:

> In the same way, those who man the lifeboat do not ask credentials from the crew of a sinking ship; they launch their boat, risk their lives in the raging waves, and somewhat perish, all to save men whom they do not even know. And what need to know them? "They are human beings, and they need our aid—that is enough, that establishes their right—To the rescue!"[28]

This is for us a familiar scene. Refugee Rescue, a nonprofit organization, and its boat *Mo Chara*, has been rescuing refugees since 2015.[29] We witnessed on June 29, 2019, Carola Rackete, captain of *Sea-Watch 3*, a boat belonging to Sea-Watch, a German nongovernmental organization, defying Italian Laws that criminalize rescue operations, rescuing forty-two migrants, and taking them to Lambedusa (Italy).[30] Similarly, Médecins Sans Frontières (MSF) or Doctors without Borders, a nonprofit and self-governed organization made up of health carers and administrators, provides medical assistance in war zones, disaster zones, as well as to refugees. Ordinary citizens also engage in practices of mutual aid. In 2015, inhabitants of the island of Lesvos run to the rescue of refugees.[31] They were even nominated for the Nobel

Peace Prize in 2016. In the art world in the UK, the Precarious Workers Brigade (BWB), a nonhierarchical association of art teachers/practitioners, runs campaigns successfully challenging the common practice of unpaid internships.[32] Kropotkin was not wrong to identify a strong mutual aid and communistic attitude within early capitalistic societies. As the aforementioned examples show, mutual aid, as a practice and politics, is present even in our contemporary neoliberal societies.[33]

Conclusion

While mutual aid may be part of our society, we may wonder how it finds its way into the arts, and dance in particular. We can imagine dancers forming nonprofit nonhierarchical associations. In *The Conquest of Bread*, Kropotkin explicitly talks about art in society. While he considers arts a luxury, he also expects that once the laboring working hours are further reduced (five hours a day for five days a week for five months a year), individuals will have at their disposal five to seven hours a day to enjoy and be involved in arts. I would imagine that dance will be one of those arts that we can engage with. And he expects "[t]housands of associations would undertake to supply them. . . . What is now the privilege of an insignificant minority would be accessible to all. Luxury, ceasing to be a foolish and ostentatious display of the bourgeois class, would become an artistic pleasure."[34] Once questions of survival are addressed through the abolition of the wage system, then access to art and dance will become, as he suggests, not a privilege but a possibility to all. Access can be access in enjoying the arts or being part of them.

Neoliberalism, Paramana and Gonzalez noted, has detrimentally affected dance and dancers by making dance less accessible.[35] To my mind, dancers, as they already rely on each other for support to bring to fruition their performances, already practice mutual aid. The challenge that Kropotkin's theory of mutual aid offers to dance is to imagine that support proliferating across all areas of one's life. If we want a world where equality, accessibility, and freedom are the core indexes, then Kropotkin's mutual aid theory opens the way to such a possibility.

Notes

1 Giorgio Agamben, "Notes on Gesture," in *Means without Ends: Notes on Politics* (Minneapolis and London: University of Minnesota Press, 2000), 49–60.

2 Ibid., 56, 57.

3 Ibid., 57, 58. Giorgio Agamben has argued that the differentiation of biological life and political life that characterized Western metaphysical thought introduced by Aristotle through his distinction of the two words that exist in Greek for life, *zoe* (biological) and *bios* (political), does not hold today. Any politics that tries to differentiate *bare life* or *zoe* from political life is by definition a totalizing politics, a politics that excludes (women, People of Color, senses) and totalizes the organization of life through particular ends, let's say economic.

4 Wendy Brown, *Undoing the Demos. Neoliberalism's Stealth Revolution* (Cambridge, MA: MIT Press, 2015).

5 Emma Goldman, *Living My Life, Vol. 1* (New York: Dover Publications, Inc., 1970), 56.

6 Ibid.

7 Emma Goldman, "Anarchism: What It Really Stands For," in *Anarchism and Other Essays* (New York: Dover Publications, Inc., 1969), 47–67.

8 Ibid., 50.

9 Ibid.

10 Goldman, *Living My Life, Vol. 1*, 56.

11 Katerina Paramana, "Performance, Dance and Political Economy: A Provocation," this volume.

12 Anita Gonzalez, "Recognizing Race and Class in Dance: Gonzalez Response to Paramana," this volume.

13 Peter Kropotkin, *Mutual Aid: A Factor of Evolution* (London: Freedom Press, 2009).

14 Peter Kropotkin, *The Conquest of Bread* (Milton Keynes: Penguin Books, 2015).

15 Kropotkin, *Mutual Aid*, 29–30.

16 Ibid.

17 Ibid., 43–4.

18 Ibid., 209.

19 Saidiya Hartman, *Wayward Lives: Beautiful Experiment* (London: Serpent's Tail, 2019). Hartman writes that Esther Brown, one of the women that her research project focused upon, disliked the slavery of waged work, especially domestic waged work. However, Brown was able to "pic[k] up work when she was in a pinch" (p. 233) because of the support she had

from her sister and grandmother as well as friends and dates. This, for Hartman, like Kropotkin, is mutual aid.

20 Kropotkin, *The Conquest of Bread*.
21 Peter Marshall, *Demanding the Impossible: A History of Anarchism* (London: Fontana Press, 1993), 325.
22 Ibid., 327.
23 Kropotkin, *The Conquest of Bread*, 27.
24 Ibid.
25 Ibid., 30.
26 Ibid.
27 Ibid.
28 Ibid., 33.
29 Refugee Rescue. http://www.refugeerescue.co.uk. Accessed September 6, 2019.
30 *African Times* editor, "Judge Releases Sea Watch Captain Who Landed Migrants at Italian Port." *African Times*, July 7, 2019. https://africatimes.com/2019/07/02/judge-releases-sea-watch-captain-who-landed-migrants-at-italian-port/. Accessed September 6, 2019.
31 Roland Schoenbauer, "Volunteers Who Saved Lives on Lesvos Nominated for Nobel Peace Prize," UNCHCR the UN Refugee Agency, October 7, 2016. https://www.unhcr.org/uk/news/latest/2016/10/57f7732d4/volunteers-saved-lives-lesvos-nominated-nobel-peace-prize.html. Accessed September 6, 2019.
32 Precarious Workers Brigade, *Training for Exploitation?: Politicising Employability & Reclaiming Education* (London, Leipzig, Los Angeles: Journal of Aesthetics & Protest Press, 2017).
33 During the Covid-19 Pandemic the UK has seen the creation of over 100 mutual aid groups. The groups were set up to support vulnerable and elderly citizens with their everyday needs. See Freedom News, "Covid-19 UK Mutual Aid Groups: A List," March 13, 2020. https://freedomnews.org.uk/covid-19-uk-mutual-aid-groups-a-list/. Accessed April 22, 2020.
34 Kropotkin, *The Conquest of Bread*, 112.
35 Paramana and Gonzalez, this volume.

DIALOGUE 6
ESCAPING CAPITALISM?

Usva Seregina, in "Breaking the Illusion of Reality: Exploring Reiterations of the Performance of Consumption", unpicks the difficulties of freeing ourselves from the logic of consumption as our everyday performances are always based on existing norms. Elena Loizidou's chapter, "From Exchange to Freedom and Back. No Guarantees," considers how mutual aid and support can be repeated throughout all spheres of life. It proposes that anarchism offers pathways to accomplish this. The chapters in Dialogue 6 question the possibility of escaping the current political and economic model and its norms, and propose ways we can succeed.

13 BREAKING THE ILLUSION OF REALITY

EXPLORING REITERATIONS OF THE PERFORMANCE OF CONSUMPTION

Usva Seregina

(A Response to the Editors' Provocations)

The contemporary world has become inundated with the logic of consumption. Specifically, in Western countries ruled by an ideology of neoliberalism, the logic of a free market seeps from traditionally commercial settings into all contexts of life, causing individuals to continuously take on the role of a consumer in order to engage with the world. Such a structure has often been called a consumer society.[1] Consumer society emerged as a result of various economic, technological, and social developments and is maintained through the actions of involved parties, including companies, governments, nation-states, and communities. One central way that individuals contribute to the perpetuation of consumer society is by performing consumption, that is, by continuously (and mostly unconsciously) enacting consumption-based power structures and consumer roles. In this chapter, I discuss how individuals perform consumption as part of everyday life and explore how dance can contribute to the break of the normalized repetition of such performance.

Consumption as a Freedom and a Constraint

Consumption, unlike its stereotypical connotations would suggest, is not merely the purchase of products or services, and it is not defined solely through materiality.[2] The act of consumption is an act of appropriation of something; a type of power structure, which always involves a consumer and a commodity that is being consumed. Consumption emerges as evaluating and making choices through which various wants, needs, and desires become defined within our society. We consume meanings rather than things, which results in a complex system of what various commodities represent in our culture, with consumption becoming the way we engage with and understand our world.[3] The logic of consumption consequently ends up defining how we interact not only with objects and services that are up for sale, but also with the context that we live in and with the people around us.[4]

Following the former logic, consumption does not necessarily need to be mass-produced or company-driven, as the consumer role and consumption logic can arise in a multitude of contexts, including the use of public goods. For example, take a look at how higher education is being reformulated in many Western countries.[5] Students have become demanding customers and lecturers are treated as service providers who need to gain the approval of their customer base. Knowledge, in such a setting, turns into a commodity to be bought rather than an educational endeavor to be taken on. Similar power structures of consumption can be seen in the way health services are being provided.[6] Treatment of health issues becomes a matter of efficiency and standardization, rather than individualized care. Patients are treated like customers, while health checks are seen by patients and doctors alike as a service commodity that can be evaluated and mass-produced.

Consumption further becomes the way that we define and place ourselves in the world. Consumption-based identity-building does not mean that everyone's identity is based on a specific range of brands that they use and display (although, this also definitely happens). Such a logic is rather seen in how we construct ourselves by freely choosing and appropriating meaning from a variety of external sources, such as products, services, communities, and spaces. The reason that this logic has gained so much traction is that it is closely intertwined with the liberal concept of freedom. This logic was intended to free individuals from the restraining class structures that previously defined how one should behave and represent oneself. Following this, to be a consumer is ultimately considered to have the freedom to make one's own choices and (at least in theory) the freedom to define one's own identity, values, and communities. Each act of consumption hence becomes not just a matter of fulfilling one's needs and desires, but of representing one's identity, place in the world, political beliefs, values, morals, and ethics.[7]

Freedom through consumption has, unfortunately, not emerged in its ideal form: we have become restrained by the forces that were meant to free us. This is most clearly visible in the inequalities inherent to consumption. In addition to giving us freedom, the consumer role was intended to make us all equal, because as consumers we all have equal access to goods and services, and thus also to the meaning- and value-making structures.[8] Yet while we are all free and equal as consumers, we do not all have equal access to *being consumers*, for there are still great class, race, gender, age, ability, and sexual orientation inequalities. For example, we do not have similar access to loans. Credit was a tool ultimately designed to allow us more access to consumption, thus making the marketplace equally accessible to all. Yet getting a loan may become impossible if one is not seen as a "desirable" client (and thus not a good commodity to invest in) by banks. This reflects issues of unequal access to dance expressed by Anita Gonzalez in her text.[9]

Consumption decisions have become increasingly complex in an age when all meaning endlessly fragments. Contemporary consumer society is driven by individuals' desire for the new and the marketplace's (the context for these desires) aim to grow and develop endlessly. Yet, as little physical or conceptual space is left for growth, meaning is forced to implode in on itself, thus fragmenting. Fragmentation sets in as a way to ensure the emergence of new meanings for consumption and to provide a basis for more and more specific self-definition.[10] Reflecting what Katerina Paramana writes in her provocation text on the intertwined nature of economic, political, and ethical decisions, consumption meanings become intertwined with cultural meanings.[11] As already discussed, each consumption choice also becomes a political, ethical, and economic one. Consequently, each choice turns out to be overwhelming, as the tiniest of decisions can have a myriad of repercussions for one's self and community, as well as the values attached to both. For instance, buying a pair of shoes is no longer just a matter of making walking more comfortable for oneself, as it rather becomes a matter of taste, status, and class. Choice of brand can further imply what trends one follows, what celebrities one admires, how environmentally aware one is, or with what politics one agrees.

Through becoming consumers, we also inadvertently commoditize ourselves.[12] Caught in a culture based on the logic of free markets, in which the main way to engage with things, values, ideas, and people is through an act of appropriation, we are pushed to objectify and distance ourselves in order to become available to the world. In other words, we turn into commodities both for ourselves and for others to consume. Our self-commodification can, for instance, be seen in the ways we value our own time and energy: we tend to think of our value in terms of labor, resources or time spent, and economic or cultural capital gained. To continue the example of higher education, as students consume "university services," they also ultimately become commodities created and consumed not only by the university, but also by the government that measures employment and education as well as institutions aiming to employ graduates. Students become the carefully measured and analyzed output of universities, which, in turn, are measured as institutions for how well they have provided a service to these commodities. Knowledge and skills are put on a conveyer belt, with ratings and surveys becoming the most valued measurement for what constitutes a good education.

As it becomes apparent, consumption emerges as a central *impediment* to individual freedom.[13] Can one get away from the logic of consumption? Many have tried to make an "escape" from market-driven contexts by using a variety of resistance tactics, such as consumer boycott, collaborative consumption, and the sharing economy.[14] These are worthwhile attempts that have had clear impact on the environment as well as on human and animal well-being. However, such escape attempts are still operating within the logic of consumption and are thus always feeding back into a consumption-driven society. Many researchers have thus suggested that escape from consumer society is impossible because of our deep acculturation into its logic.[15]

Perhaps it is pointless to ask whether or not we can be free of the logic of consumption. Any reinterpreted performance of everyday life will always be based on existing norms in some form, as we cannot constitute a reality outside of what we know.[16] However, what we *can do* and, more importantly, what *dance can help us do* is become aware of the power structures guiding and building our reality, as this allows for the slow dismantling of the acculturated normative reiteration of performances.

To help me outline my suggestions for how we can break free of norms of reality set by consumption, I discuss two issues present in contemporary consumption-driven society that I believe need to be addressed urgently and which are well suited for exploration through dance. The first issue is the widespread unawareness of consumption-driven norms as a major structuring element of society, and the second issue is a loss of bodily connection between individuals and the world. I begin by situating this chapter more concretely in the perspective of performance.

Performing Everyday Life

Performance, following Schechner, is a behavior that is restored through "recombining bits of previously behaved behaviors."[17] In other words, our performance of everyday life is based on repeating and recombining bits of performances that have been performed previously. Performances are not exact and thus change over time, creating the norms and structures of our society, although never in themselves becoming those rules. Our understanding of performance is based on their past repetitions, which form our history and create an authority of norms that structures how we act.[18] The performance of consumption, I would argue, has become the prevalent form of performing everyday life, with individuals becoming largely blind to the types of performances they are recreating. These structures nevertheless define who we are as individuals, communities, and societies.

From a performance point of view, it becomes interesting to explore not whether things are repeated (as they inadvertently are), but *how* things are repeated.[19] In this light, I believe it is important to deconstruct *how* consumption is performed, as well as how it structures and maintains the social world in which we live today.

Blindness to Norms

The first issue that I suggest dance can help address is our unawareness of how consumption-driven our lives are, which is mainly due to the normalization of everyday life. As we enact similar performances inundated with power structures of consumption over and over, we form our reality, the understanding of which we are acculturated into through conventions and repeated experiences. The structures created through these repetitions are seen as normal, forming our knowledge and belief about our world. Simultaneously, we become blind to these structures, as normalized repetition requires no reflection or conscious thought. Because norms are felt to be innate, we come to experience them as preexisting their performance; fixed and unalterable.[20] Consumption-driven reality thus feels natural and normal because we have made it so by enacting its structures, with any alternative seemingly impossible.

Normative structures emerge with a multitude of functions in our society. On the one hand, norms bind and govern life, constraining us and thus blinding us to the option of repeating performances differently or even not repeating them at all. On the other hand, they guide us in our behavior and help us understand the world around us. Moreover, while norms precede performance, they are also recreated each time they are enacted, with each performance never being repeated exactly. Performances are therefore unstable and can involve any level on interpretation, misinterpretation, and even failure. This creates the possibility of agency, which is not control over a performance, but rather the failure of its iterability.[21] This is where, I believe, dance can play an important role in engaging in a conversation about the power structures of consumer society.

From a perspective of performance, dance can be seen as a type of aesthetic performance. Following Turner and Schechner, aesthetic performance differs from everyday performance in that it is highly conscious and can extend reality because it does not need to be situated within its norms.[22] Norms within aesthetic performance are less fixed, yet much more visible, making what seems impossible a possibility. As a result, aesthetic performance is perfect for making visible, commenting on, or questioning existing structures, because it can shed light on problems that would go unnoticed as a result of the routinized repetition of norms in everyday life. In this sense, dance can become a way of breaking the illusion of both the fixed nature of our reality and the inalterability of norms set within a consumerist mindset, by causing us to consciously act in nonnormative ways. Dance can push individuals to have deep awareness of both the performance being engaged, as no existing blueprint can be used for its basis, and of the norms of everyday life, because these have to clearly overstepped. As a result, individuals become highly aware and self-aware, which causes them to reflect on and better understand their selves and the world around them. Many other art forms similarly allow for reflection and self-awareness, but not necessarily in a bodily manner, as I discuss next.

Losing Bodily Connection

The second issue dance can help address is one of the loss of bodily connection with our environment. In commoditizing ourselves and focusing on individual needs, we lose solidarity with one another in consumption-driven culture, which causes our connections to other people and to our contexts to become weaker. In continuously enacting performances of consumption, we inevitably make ourselves both a consumer and a commodity, thus objectifying ourselves, as noted earlier. Commodities need to be accessible and equal to all despite their background, and hence must be uprooted and disconnected from any context that ties them down to a meaning in a way that is too particular. At the same time, a consumer society promotes an individual's freedom to choose their own identity and place in society. Culture becomes oriented at the individual and their personal needs and desires, making community less of a powerful normative structure.

Schechner proposes that individuals were not always disconnected, with culture being previously much more community-oriented.[23] He discusses the idea of performance knowledge, which is the transmission of shared meaning through bodily face-to-face interactions. He stresses that this was the main form of knowledge transfer in traditional, preindustrial communities, but is largely lost to contemporary culture, in which we learn about our world largely through text and imagery. The latter forms have become prioritized in representing knowledge, with their power being closely tied to the values of a consumption-driven society. Text and images capture knowledge in rational, regulated, and clearly recorded forms that have objective and seemingly neutral truth value.[24] As a result, individuals feel that their interpretation of knowledge is correct and unalterable, even as a variety of perspectives persist. Knowledge becomes solidified, commodified, and prepackaged, thus lacking experiential, emotional, and bodily value.

We become used to prepackaged knowledge, expecting to consume knowledge in the way we would consume a candy bar. This is an issue that every lecturer faces in today's classroom, as exemplified in Anita Gonzalez's discussion of her students' unwillingness to reflect on issues or question their realities.[25] We are no longer accustomed to or acculturated into interaction that pushes us to find meaning together and thus construct our individual knowledge as part of a collective endeavor. We rather expect to receive knowledge only in the form of information: directly, immediately, and without work put into it.

Yet knowledge can emerge in many other forms, engaging the world in ways other than the rational, the recorded, the regulated, and the objective. Dance is one way that knowledge can be created through emotion, sensation, as well as bodily interaction with space, with objects, and with other people. Dance can thus become a way for individuals to engage in performance knowledge: knowledge that emerges through learning from body to body, through connecting to one another and to the world in a physical, spatial manner. It becomes a matter of engaging different types of knowledge and thus tapping into bodily understandings that we normally do not consciously reflect on or even have access to.[26]

Breaking the Illusion of Reality

How is it that we can become aware of the performance of consumption? How can we reflect on the fact that we enact the roles of consumers? What emerges most importantly in the discussion on the topic of dance and the power structures of consumer society is the ability of dance to break the repetition of the performance of reality, forcing us to reconsider the fixed nature of reality and knowledge. As Borden has stressed, spaces and norms cannot be changed in themselves, but our engagement with them can be. He adds that by using and interacting with spaces in previously unintended ways, we engage in lived critique, a very conscious act of understanding one's reality.[27] Through becoming aware of how we perform reality, we come to understand its constructed nature, gaining insight into how our actions and interactions contribute to building structures of power and oppression. Moreover, we obtain the ability to either stop performing elements of normalized performance or to repeat them in different ways. By engaging the world both in a rational, reflexive manner and via bodily, emotional interaction, dance can allow us to gain understanding of how it is that we enact consumer society and its power structures, as well as give us a direction for exploring new possibilities for building a future together.

Importantly, dance can further get us back in touch with our own bodies, thus reestablishing a connection between ourselves and the world, which is necessary for building solidarity and connections to others. This would allow us to reengage with performance knowledge and pull our resources together in order to gain momentum in changing our performances of reality. Contemporary society pushes us to be individuals and hence cuts us off from everyone else, diminishing our chances of making a difference, as an individual always has less power than a group. By finding one another, we gain a greater ability to become aware of, break, and rebuild existing power structures of a consumption-oriented reality.[28]

Notes

1 Don Slater, *Consumer Culture and Modernity* (Oxford: Polity Press, 1997); Zygmunt Bauman, *Consuming Life* (Cambridge: Polity Press, 2007).

2 Lizbeth Cohen, *A Consumers Republic: The Politics of Mass Consumption in Postwar America* (New York: Knopf, 2003); Eric Arnould, "Should Consumer Citizens Escape the Market?" *The Annals of the American Academy of Political and Social Science* 1, no. 611 (2007): 96–111.

3 Jean Baudrillard, *The Consumer Society* (London: Sage, 1998).

4 Slater, *Consumer Culture and Modernity*.

5 For example, in *The Death of Expertise: The Campaign Against Established Knowledge and Why It Matters* (Oxford: Oxford University Press, 2017), Tom Nichols discusses the commodification of higher education in the UK.

6 For example, in *Against Creativity* (London: Verso Books, 2018), Oli Mould provides a perspective on the commodification of UK's National Health Service (NHS) in the context of creativity.

7 Fuat Firat and Alladi Venkatesh, "Liberatory Postmodernism and the Reenchantment of Consumption," *Journal of Consumer Research*, 3, no. 22 (1995): 239–67; Slater, *Consumer Culture and Modernity*; Bauman, *Consuming Life*.

8 Slater, *Consumer Culture and Modernity*.

9 Anita Gonzalez, "Recognizing Race and Class in Dance: Gonzalez Response to Paramana," this volume.

10 Baudrillard, *The Consumer Society*.

11 Katerina Paramana, "Performance, Dance and Political Economy: A Provocation," this volume.

12 Bauman, *Consuming Life*.

13 Firat and Venkatesh, "Liberatory Postmodernism and the Reenchantment of Consumption."

14 Arnould, "Should Consumer Citizens Escape the Market?"; Rob Kozinets, "Can Consumers Escape the Market? Emancipatory Illuminations from Burning Man," *Journal of Consumer Research* 1, no. 29 (2002): 20–38.

15 Colin Campbell, *The Romantic Ethic and the Spirit of Modern Consumerism* (Oxford: Basil Blackwell Ltd., 1987); Slater, *Consumer Culture and Modernity*; Bauman, *Consuming Life*.

16 Judith Butler, *Gender Trouble: Feminism and the Subversion of Identity* (New York: Routledge, 1990).

17 Richard Schechner, *Performance Studies. An Introduction* (Abingdon: Routledge, 2006), 35.

18 Victor Turner, *On the Edge of the Bush: Anthropology as Experience* (Tucson: The University of Arizona Press, 1985); Schechner, *Performance Studies. An Introduction*.

19 Marvin Carlson, *Performance: A Critical Introduction*, Second edition (London: Routledge, 2003).

20 Schechner, *Performance Studies. An Introduction.*

21 Judith Butler, *Undoing Gender* (New York: Routledge, 2004).

22 Turner, *On the Edge of the Bush: Anthropology as Experience*; Schechner, *Performance Studies. An Introduction.*

23 Richard Schechner, *Performance Theory* (New York: Routledge, 1982).

24 Susan Finley, "Arts-Based Inquiry in QI: Seven Years from Crisis to Guerrilla Warfare," *Qualitative Inquiry* 2, no. 9 (2003): 281–96; Victoria Scotti and Angela Libby Aicher, "Veiling and Unveiling: An Artistic Exploration of Self-Other Processes," *Qualitative Inquiry,* 3, no. 22 (2015): 192–7.

25 Gonzalez, "Recognizing Race and Class in Dance: Gonzalez Response to Paramana."

26 For more on art-based knowledge, see Usva Seregina, "Co-creating Bodily, Interactive, and Reflexive Knowledge Through Art-Based Research," *Consumption Markets & Culture* 23, no. 6 (2020): 513–36.

27 Iain Borden, *Skateboarding, Space and the City. Architecture and the Body* (Oxford: Oxford International Publishers Ltd., 2001).

28 Interestingly, in light of the Covid-19 pandemic, we are seeing a resurgence of focus on bodily interaction and on the other, as our normal (usually consumption-based) ways of fulfilling our needs and interacting with the world are failing. With restricted access to commodities as well as facing new patterns and schedules for life, we are having to relearn how to make and fix things. For example, more people are cooking and baking from scratch and many have to homeschool their children while working from home. Many mutual aid groups have emerged to help the elderly or marginalized groups, such as groups within the LGBTQ+ community. Mutual aid groups have been supporting those who are vulnerable in ways that governments or local authorities are unable to, for example, by helping with shopping for groceries or getting medication. In the context of the pandemic, we are thus realizing our deep dependence on others as well as our normalized reliance on consumer society. What will we be able to take forward and learn from this global event?

14 FROM EXCHANGE TO FREEDOM AND BACK
NO GUARANTEES
Elena Loizidou

(A Response to Videos From the Playlist[1])

Anarchism is the social and political philosophy that calls for the abolition of the state, rules, and authority and consequently proposes political economic associations that reflect these ideas. I consider Kropotkin's[2] political economy of mutual aid a pathway to such society. I speculate that dance may have something to teach anarchism about mutual aid; after all, dancers support one another during performances—both physically and by "listening" to and working collaboratively with one another to support the ideas of the work.

Katerina Paramana and Anita Gonzalez asked us to consider and discuss how two performances/public events—one of our choosing and another suggested by other contributors to this book—address the relation between performance/dance (in its broadest conception) and political economy. I write about Merce Cunningham's *Exchange* (1978) and Ebony Noelle Golden's *125th and Freedom: Public Performance Ritual* (2017). Cunningham, I will suggest, used anarchist techniques in the *creation* and *staging* of his choreographies. His work *Exchange*, in particular, tells us something about the nature of exchange in our world and provides us with a better understanding of how mutual aid can work. Golden's performance invokes the idea of freedom, which is at the core of anarchism. Anarchism calls for freeing ourselves from conventions[3] and rules, as well as for willingly becoming members of mutual aid associations. My aim here is to see to what extent these two choreographies can teach anarchism something about creating an anarchist world.

Exchange

Cunningham, one of the most renowned modern dance choreographers, is interpolated by some as an anarchist.[4] Anna Kisselgoff provides us with this image in an interview she conducted with him in 1992.[5] In the interview, Kisselgoff identifies the main anarchist characteristic of his choreographies as playfulness. Anarchism, as I have already indicated, repudiates conventionalism—which bleeds joy out of life—encourages playfulness, and requires the refutation of certain institutions such as the state and principles such as authority. Cunningham created a dance company that bears his name (Merce Cunningham Dance Company[6]), an indication of his symbolic attachment to mastery and hierarchy. Although, then, Cunningham's anarchy was *not* anarchism, nevertheless, his work could still teach us something about mutual aid.

Cunningham explains that he had no objective in mind before creating a dance[7] and often used chance procedures. This idea of having no blueprint is also at the heart of anarchist thinking (no rules). Therefore, Cunningham's anarchism, I suggest, can be observed in the methods he used to compose a choreography. I look at one of his earlier pieces, *Exchange* (1978), to see to what extent Cunningham's techniques were anarchic and what his interpretation of exchange could contribute to anarchism.

Exchange is described by David Vaugham as belonging "in the category . . . of . . . Cunningham's epic work."[8] It is forty minutes long, divided in three sections, and accompanied by music composed by David Tudor. The first part is danced in a circular manner "by the more recent recruits"[9] of the Company, the second diagonally by the older members, and the third by both groups coming together. The dancers move independently of Tudor's soundtrack.[10] The choreography, in its variation in movement (circularly, diagonally, together) and distance from David Tudor's music, I suggest provides a vision of how a mutual aid polity may look like. It teaches that a polity built upon mutual aid requires our *coming together* with both our differences—psychic, material, and structural—and similarities (i.e., vulnerability) to create something new. The use of alternative positions (signified by the different shapes of movement) in the work provides us with a visual/moving composition of *how* we can come together to achieve this. Moreover, as the dancers move to the rhythm of their bodies ignoring the soundtrack—a soundtrack that mimics the noises and rhythms of a busy capitalist city—they carry along the hopeful message of the possibility of escaping the harsh rhythms of our capitalist world. In this way, the work gestures toward the building of something new *despite* the rhythms of capitalism.

So, if *Exchange* has something to teach anarchism, it is that mutual aid requires attention to difference and freeing ourselves from the rhythms and sounds of capitalism. Moreover, it appears that some instinctive idea about mutual aid was also at the back of Cunningham's mind when using chance as a choreographic methodology. Chance, he explained, generates a sense of awareness among dancers:

> I think they're aware of it, because even if you are only dancing apart, after a while, you begin, if you're at all conscious, to develop a sense about what the others are doing, and you realize they're doing something else. You have to begin to know where the other dancer is, without looking. It has to do with time, the relationship with the timing. If you paid attention to the timing, then even if you weren't facing them, you knew they were there. And that made a relationship. It depends also on how you think something can be created, too. If you always think that relationships are only one way, then that's the way you do it. But if you think relationships can be many ways, then that comes into your possible perception. It's like a cat. It doesn't have to turn around and look at something, it knows it's there. In human beings, it comes by experience, and certainly my pieces develop this faculty.[11]

Cunningham alerts us to the human ability of building a world, or as in his case a choreography, without the need of a script, but instead by simply being aware of each others' movements and relating accordingly. Awareness of each others' movements enables us to also support each other's work in a mutually beneficial manner. I suppose he is saying that there is an instinct that enables us to relate to one another and exchange without destroying one another.

Despite Cunningham's shortfalls (i.e., attachment to recognition that he is a master choreographer), *Exchange* enables us to see how space can be reorganized so as to recognize *equality* among the dancers and include movements created by *chance* that carry our *different* rhythms. Chance movement releases us from the constrained movements of capitalism captured by the soundscape of the work.

FIGURE 5 *Exchange* choreographed by Merce Cunningham (1978). Merce Cunningham Dance © Lois Greenfield.

125th and Freedom

Ebony Noelle Golden's 2017 dance *125th and Freedom* is a street performance, procession, and re-occupation of space that takes place on 125th Street between the Hudson and Harlem rivers. The choreography is made out of ten *choreopoetic* rituals that are performed over five hours. The work honors the radical traditions of 125th Street (Harlem), The Great Migration, and The Underground Railroad[12] and offers both a critique of our sociopolitical terrain and a creative way of exiting the political, economic, and social inequalities that plague us. It is powerful to see these thirty dancers, made up of an array of activists, moving through and remarking our public spaces, singing, reading poetry, and chanting, among other chants, "Black Is Freedom." Golden's choreography reveals that, while our freedom is restricted and our spaces are narrowed down by capitalism, authoritarian regimes, and cultural prejudices, we can break through those limits if we listen to the rhythms of change (some paradoxically coming from the past). We can free ourselves if, we listen to rhythms that we hold inside our bodies and if, we unite, irrespective of abilities and experience. Freedom requires or even demands the hands, voices, and memories of all. The slogan "Make Waves" is written on belts worn by dancers. As a sea of mostly women moves in circles, we can sense what the chant "Make Waves" anticipates: change. A change that cannot be achieved just by singular individuals but instead requires the energy and force of all;[13] it requires the rhythm of all. Accompanying the dancers are sounds of drumming, megaphones, and the voices of the performers. These succeed in drowning city noises. They succeed in showing us how to free ourselves from the noise of capitalism.

Moreover, Golden's choreopoetic *125th and Freedom* achieves what Cunningham *Exchange* does not and may not be able to ever achieve. Paramana[14] and Gonzalez tell us of the limitations of dance.[15] One such limitation is its affordability and accessibility to lower socioeconomic groups. When dance takes place in public spaces, on our streets, our parks, our roads, when the dancers and singers and poets are not professional dancers, then the question of economic inequality and participation to dance becomes addressed. When *movement* is aligned with solidarity and support, when *rhythm* springs from our very collective gestures and songs, then mutual aid is not an aspiration; it is a way of life and freedom. Golden's powerful *choreopoetics* evidences that the practice of mutual aid does not lay anymore in the private confines of the stage but makes the world its stage.

Paramana and Gonzalez have asked us to imagine together what performance/dance and movement can tell us about political economy and vice versa. In embarking in this journey I learned what dance and movement lend to anarchist thinking and what anarchism can learn from dance. This has been an invaluable exchange, an unforgettable experience of interdisciplinary engagement for which I am grateful.

Notes

1 Merce Cunningham, *Exchange*, 1978. https://youtu.be/ciBqm_XtYVE, accessed September 12, 2019. Ebony Noelle Golden, *125th and Freedom: Public Performance Ritual* (highlight reel), 2017, https://www.youtube.com/watch?v=-rXPt2wHzoE, accessed September 12, 2019.

2 Peter Kropotkin, *Mutual Aid: A Factor of Evolution* (London: Freedom Press, 2009). In *Mutual Aid* Kropotkin suggests that it is mutual aid and not competition that is the most dominant instinct in the human and animal world. In *The Conquest of Bread* (Milton Keynes: Penguin Books, 2015), Peter Kropotkin explains how mutual aid societies are made up of individuals that join freely and are organized on the basis of two principles: (1) abolition of private property and (2) remuneration according to people's needs.

3 Emma Goldman, *Living My Life, Vol. 1* (New York: Dover Publications, Inc., 1970), 56.

4 Anna Kisselgoff, "DANCE; Merce Cunningham, Explorer and Anarchist," *The New York Times,* March 15, 1992. https://www.nytimes.com/1992/03/15/arts/dance-merce-cunningham-explorer-and-anarchist.html, accessed August 20, 2019.

5 Ibid.

6 Cunningham was less attached to hierarchy, a principle (i.e. the dismantling of hierarchies) that is at the heart of anarchism. This is evidenced by the fact that he lists the dancers of each performance alphabetically and not by some other criteria which would have set one dancer apart from the rest.

7 Kisselgoff, "DANCE: Merce Cunningham, Explorer and Anarchist."

8 David Vaughan, "Merce Cunningham: Retrospect and Prospect," *Performing Arts Journal* 3, no. 3 (Winter 1979): 3–14, at 11.

9 Vaughan, "Merce Cunningham: Retrospect and Prospect."

10 Cunningham is quoted saying that with *Exchange* he wanted to show the slight differences in the repetitions of gestures, words, and ideas; see Merce Cunningham Trust, *Exchange*, http://www.mercecunningham.org/the-work/choreography/exchange/, accessed September 12, 2019.

11 Merce Cunningham, *The Dancer and the Dance* (London and New York: Marion Boayars, 2009), 23.

12 Between 1916 and 1970 African Americans were moving from the South to other parts of the United States such as the West. This migration—known as the Great Migration—was a response to Jim Crow's racist laws. The Underground Railroad refers to secret routes that enslaved Black Americans took in the nineteenth century to reach states where slavery had been abolished. Harlem in the 1920s saw the arrival of the largest population of African Americans during the Great Migration and a renaissance of cultural and artistic activities. *125th and Freedom* reminds us that the flourishing culture of Harlem has been built by African Americans who escaped the racist laws of the South but moreover that freedom requires constant struggle.

13 In the UK during the Covid-19 pandemic, we have seen more than 100 Mutual Aid Groups emerging all over the country, evidence of Kropotkin's position that mutual support is essential for our survival (https://covidmutualaid.org).

14 Katerina Paramana, "Performance, Dance and Political Economy: A Provocation," this volume.

15 Anita Gonzalez, "Recognizing Race and Class in Dance: Gonzalez Response to Paramana," this volume.

GROUP CONVERSATION

Group Conversation

15 IN CONVERSATION – PERFORMANCE, DANCE AND POLITICAL ECONOMY

BODIES AT THE END OF THE WORLD

Katerina Paramana, Anita Gonzalez, Nina Power, Marc Arthur, Melissa Blanco Borelli, Usva Seregina, Jamila Johnson-Small, Elena Loizidou, and Alexandrina Hemsley

Transcribed by Anne Hickley
Edited and Introduced by Katerina Paramana

The final dialogical exchange among the book's contributors was a live group conversation, which took place on 23 March 2020. It aimed at furthering our previous exchanges and creating space for reflection on our writing and concerns until that point in time. To do this, Anita and I paired each essay with that of another contributor and asked that they prepare a three-mins oral response to it. These responses were to be shared with everyone at our group meeting and serve as starting points for wider discussion. (The responses were to each author's second essay drafts—unlike the group meeting, these drafts preceded most of the Covid-19 lockdowns.) The pairing of the essays, resulting in six dialogical exchanges, was based on specific points by each author that made an impression on us and which we thought could dialogue in a fruitful manner with those of another author. The reasons for the pairings are articulated within the conversation.

Group Conversation, 23 March 2020 (via Zoom)

Key (in order of speaking):

KP = Katerina Paramana

AG = Anita Gonzalez

NP = Nina Power

MA = Marc Arthur

MBB = Melissa Blanco Borelli

US = Usva Seregina

JJ-S = Jamila Johnson-Small

EL = Elena Loizidou

AH = Alexandrina Hemsley (video recording)

Var = Various people together

An informal conversation and checking in with one another under the challenging Covid-19 circumstances preceded the video recording. Katerina, Elena, Usva, Jamila, and Alexandrina participated from the UK; Anita, Melissa, and Marc from the US; and Nina from Spain.

KP: Thank you for joining us during these very difficult times. For the purposes of the recording, today is the twenty-third of March 2020. At this point in time, unlike Greece and many other countries, the US and the UK are not yet on lockdown—but we shall see.

Our conversation today will be unavoidably affected by Covid-19, which I believe has made perfectly clear how capitalist economies determine how a problem is addressed and also who is most affected by it. The pandemic has also revealed both the problematic priorities, approaches, and policies of neoliberal capitalism and also the importance of socialist approaches such as free healthcare for all and universal basic income.

Your writing for this book has become even more poignant under the circumstances—re-reading today, for example, Melissa's text on endings, which is part of the document with the dialogical pairs I shared with you earlier today, hit me quite hard. Your essays have offered wonderful points and reflections and, although we have paired them in a specific way this time around, there are many ways in which they echo and comment on one another. If you haven't already, I would like to ask you to open the document I shared with you earlier, so you also have a visual reference.

The structure Anita and I have decided on for this conversation is to spend approximately four minutes on each essay.[1] I know this might be a bit too structured and we may decide to scrap it—we'll see how it goes. But we have decided for now that it may be useful, in order to further the conversations we've already had through writing, to ask each of you to offer a three-minute response to the essay of another contributor before having a discussion as a group. Anita and I will take turns sharing a summary of each of the dialogical pairs and the reasons for pairing them. Then each contributor will offer their response; any immediate responses are welcome, but we hope to have a longer discussion at the end. Let's see how it goes—we may want to make changes to the structure as things progress. So, shall we start with Dialogue 1, Anita?

AG: Yes, sounds good. **Dialogue 1**, titled ***Control of Bodies,*** is between Nina and Mark. Nina wrote about "the ways in which bodies are distributed in space: what happens when bodies are measured and captured by the state, and what happens when they are (temporarily at least) not measured or captured." Marc wrote about how bodies are violently arranged within economic agendas and ideologies of control.

KP: Perhaps it is important to also note that this is not a "summary" of your work, but points you made that made an impression on us and which we also thought would make good points of discussion in relation to those of another author.

So perhaps we can start with Nina, responding to Marc and then Marc to Nina, if that's OK?

NP: Yeah, sure. OK. Obviously the context is quite strange; it's been hard to return to work in any kind of normal way. I have also had to find somewhere to stay here (Spain) (*laughs*) which has been interesting, but successful, so far.

I was looking at Marc's second essay, which is on the *Act Up* video and *Tierra* by Galindo. Obviously in context, there's something very relevant about the question of AIDS and transmission and health, so there's an obvious, immediate response. Even before reading Marc's essay, I was thinking about the question of plague and I put together a plague list, which included works by Diamanda Galas. I'm very interested in music, so there is a sense in which I've been listening to a certain kind of, at least sonic, response to the question of plague and even interested in bringing back in a certain way this word (plague), which was obviously re-politicised during the AIDS crisis. I haven't heard too many people using the word "plague" in this current iteration of a different kind of infectious disease, but nevertheless, it is obviously a kind of perennial question biopolitically, socially, and otherwise. The thing that struck me the most about Marc's essay was a kind of desire, it seemed to me, on his part, to give rage a meaning; that is to say, to harness rage or have an optimistic reading of it, to see what happens when rage is not only performed and staged but then revisited and captured for political ends. A while ago, I was re-reading Peter Sloterdijk's book, *Rage and Time*, a very interesting text, in which he argues, at the beginning of the book, that the origins of Western civilization as it were begin with a howl of rage in *The Iliad*. And I was wondering, perhaps this is more of a question to Marc—I enjoyed his essay, it put me also in mind of Lauren Berlant's work in some ways—but I wondered about this desire to recapture rage. Is there not also a kind of rage, which perhaps we're also reliving or experiencing now, perhaps not even reliving, but a new rage in the face of perhaps a whole series of unknowables. In a way the AIDS crisis . . . can we talk about the AIDS crisis as being harnessed or captured now? Obviously, it is still an on-going question, even in the age of PrEP (Pre-Exposure Prophylaxis) and knowledge, and scientific awareness and antiretrovirals. I suppose it is a deeper question, to bring it to choreography, about an uncapturable rage: is there a rage that perhaps in an embodied way or otherwise, or a performance way, exceeds its political capturability? Is there a rage of the dying Covid body or something like this that is not recuperable in some sense for any kind of optimistic project? And perhaps this is just a reflection of a certain kind of relation to risk and uncertainty which we're all globally living through at the moment. I suppose this was my overriding feeling about this—the deep, ontological nature of rage in relation to the West and also its excessive and perhaps uncapturable quality.

AG: Thank you. Marc, do you want to respond?

MA: Thank you so much, Nina, for your feedback and thoughts. First, this idea you bring up of rage in the present has been on my mind a lot for obvious reasons. Within my own AIDS activist and scholarly communities, comparisons made between AIDS and Covid have been coming up a lot. But when people make this comparison they are often thinking about the early AIDS crisis as this distinct period, without taking into account the *on-goingness* of the crisis. Therefore, in some ways, the fact that AIDS is an on-going crisis and continues to be a pandemic is more relevant and evokes a contemporary form of AIDS-related rage. There are definitely a lot of comparisons there (AIDS was then known as "the gay disease" or virus; of course now we have some calling Covid-19 the Chinese virus . . .) but I think in my essay on rage I'm trying to think about the on-going ways in which HIV tracks inequalities along the lines of race and class. This is something we can think about in terms of relationships between HIV and Covid—how, for example, they both disproportionately impact communities of color. And also, in terms of the performance question, we can look at the embodied knowledge that gets taken up, and this includes rage, during both pandemics. How do activists and others take accountability and make decisions for their bodies in times of crisis? Of course this is complex to unravel in a moment like ours when Covid-19 is just emerging.

I'm now going to talk about your beautiful essay.

Thank you, Katerina and Anita for bringing our two pieces into conversation. Our shared interest in the possibility of a collective form of political movement was really exciting to me. I connected with a lot of your writing, Nina, and found your idea to "present the desirability of bodies becoming collective bodies without eliminating difference" powerful. The *Spatial Confessions* video, which you discuss in your essay, is a video I recently showed to a class I'm teaching on community and socially engaged performance. One of the students' first responses was to question the extent to which the museum itself limited the possibility for such engagement and also, therefore, why this work was happening in the museum at all. The students' response highlights the pernicious ways in which the museum, over the past ten years at least, has presented performance art within economies of art collection as a sort of revolutionary act. I'm thinking here, for example, of Tino Sehgal's work or Marina Abramović's retrospective at MoMA (The Museum of Modern Art, New York City). I enthusiastically agree with your reading of *Spatial Confessions* as exploding quantitative processes of political polling and measurement by taking them to an extreme. But I also wonder how we can think about the museum as this other form of measure and control, and ask whether the piece is doing something to push against institutional practices of economically-incentivized measurement.

Lastly, I was thinking about this idea that emerges in both Jeremy Deller's piece *Everybody in the Place* and in *Spatial Confessions*: that the works are framed as "dance," which you write is, "movement that is, in each case, amateur, popular, free, voluntary," and points towards "expressions of freedom." This is compelling and reminded me a bit of Judith Butler's *Notes Towards a Performative Theory Assembly*. I will do a little performative reading now. (*Laughs*)

KP: (*Laughs*)

AG: (*Laughs*)

MA: Butler writes, "In my view, a shared condition of precarity situates our political lives. If, as Adriana Cavarero has argued, the exposure of our bodies in public space constitutes us fundamentally and establishes our thinking as social and embodied, vulnerable and passionate, then our thinking gets nowhere without the presupposition of that very corporal interdependency and entwinement. The body is constituted through perspectives it cannot inhabit. Someone else sees our face in a way that we cannot and hears our voice in a way that we cannot. We are, in a sense, bodily, always over there, yet here, and this dispossession marks the sociality to which we belong."[2] So I was thinking, what is the insurgency of these two performances? This quotation makes me think it has something to do with the corporeality of bodies occupying space together—as you write in your text, Nina, "We are also in a space in multiple other ways" and you go on to list some fabulous ways this happens. I was interested in how we can explore the manner in which this live connection of collectivity and activation of bodies in space, situated both here and there, close and far, can locate us together in precarity. I think this might open questions about this very interaction we're having and the ways in which we're both very distant right now but can also find new ways to be close.

AG: Thank you for that, Marc—it was lovely. Jamila, thank you for just joining us.

We've just heard from Marc, so perhaps it would be good if we heard from Melissa and Usva now, talking about community disruptions (**Dialogue 4: *Communal Disruptions***).

KP: Yes, sounds good.

AG: We paired these two essays because of their particular approach and insights into communities. Melissa was talking about *convivencia*, which she understands in this case as the ability to coexist through dance performance. In her essay, she discusses a region in Colombia, in which communities were able to "re-member and re-choreograph themselves back into the(ir) space after histories of displacement" by staging and performing in a dance festival.

Usva was talking about aiming to disrupt existing normative structures by deconstructing familiar relationships of one's body to space, but also about the importance of presenting work with and within communities in order to "build meaning together and contextually" and address power structures. So I wondered whether, having read each other's essays, you have things that you would like to bring into the dialogue.

MBB: Sure, I'm starting right? "Melissa 1." (*Laughter*)

Well, Usva thank you for sharing your essay with me. What I was thinking about when I was reading it was the ways in which—at least in the context I'm working on currently, which is in the Afro-Colombian communities that have been affected by the paramilitary crisis—communities interact with one another and with performance. In your essay, you suggest it is important that performances/artists interact "with contexts that do not readily engage in artistic performances and wor[k] with communities and in communities by engaging individuals in dance performance they would not normally have access to." You suggest this "would allow them access to knowledge and understanding that is different from what they are used to." This made me think about a workshop we did, not specifically *with* the communities, but a workshop led by a woman who has done dance theatre work with them. What she shared with us was how, for many of the people in the community, coming back together again *as* a community is really important because of their experiences of displacement, violence, and grief for the families killed. This idea of having a comeback and sharing space in a non-threatening way and the sharing of her experiences working with them to make this theatre piece were powerful. She talked about the ways in which she would have them just put their hands on one another's shoulders, stand in a circle and make sure that they say everybody's name, and look at them in the eye; this ability to just be able to look someone in the eye and not turn away. And then it was about moving through rhythm and movement and just being able to watch one another and follow one another's movements. She would then lift up her arms and we would have to lift up our arms also, and it was . . . I'm sure many of you are thinking this is like collaborative theatre making, these kinds of applied theatre games that you do to establish a type of community. But what was interesting particularly in that context was, again, that these were people that . . . they could be a neighbor, but this neighbor had a friend who was a paramilitary, whereas that neighbor had a friend who was a victim. So it's this trying to undo these perpetrator/victim relationships through other forms of tying in the communities, particularly—at least in grant language, because it is a grant I have, they always speak about—these marginalized communities that have been affected by the military and paramilitary conflict, but at the end of the day it's really that these communities have been erased by the state; the Colombian state just doesn't care. There's no interest in terms of state investment in this part of the country, unless it's extractivist capital, right? Let's move these people away. The different contexts, then, in which community is built are very interesting to me—whether this happens through following instruction, through listening, through stepping into an unknown, through your body and trying to find a way to connect through that embodied experience, whether it's by watching closer or watching *Spatial Confessions* and inviting that kind of thinking and connection, or by being in a humid (*laughs*) space in the Pacific region of Colombia.

KP: Thank you, Melissa.

US: Yeah, thank you. It's really interesting to hear about a performance that takes on ideas similar to those I was writing about. I guess I'll just jump into my response to your essay, which I found really interesting. What I found fascinating was the context as well, because I've mainly worked in Northern Europe and a little bit in Western Europe, so I don't really know anything about the Colombian culture.

MBB: Thing is, me neither! Really! (*Laughs*)

US: Yeah, but it's still fascinating to hear about and that's what is really important about some of these performances and essays: mapping out . . . as you say as well, getting people in touch with their history, but also the rest of the world finding out about these histories that have been erased and have been pushed back, because it was decided that they're unnecessary or somehow redundant to that particular regime. But yeah, I had some similar thoughts to you. The performance you describe is such a great example of how we can share knowledge bodily and how we can learn bodily and engage histories in a non-textual and non-written way, which as I suggest in my essay is important. A lot of our contemporary, at least Western culture—and the rest of the world is Westernizing fast as well—tends to look at history through text, through language, which of course is important, but there are so many other ways of remembering, so many other ways of learning. Your case study is a really great example of how that can work and how people can get in touch with their own histories and express together in different ways. What I found really interesting is when you talked about how some of these performances are supported in a monetary way, are dependent on funding. For me, this was an interesting paradox.

MBB: Mhm, minimal funding, but funding, yeah.

US: Yeah, and so while they're pushing back, trying to get their own culture and their own history, they're still kind of bound by these other structures, which are the same structures that essentially erase their histories. Unfortunately this happens a lot throughout the world, but I think that's an interesting . . . not interesting in a good way, but an interesting idea and paradox. What does that mean, does that funding still then have an effect on how that history is presented? I don't know, but potentially it could, right? And so, what does that mean for their autonomy, if they're fighting for an autonomy but they're still being funded by these people? I think these were the main things I was responding to, but yeah, a really interesting essay, thank you.

MBB: Thank you.

KP: Thank you, both. It seems good to now have **Dialogue 3: *Rest, Productivity and Survival***, if that's OK?

ALL: (*Nods*)

KP: Great. Jamila, in her performance text, is discussing ideas of productivity, rest, fatigue, and survival. She connects them to the political and socioeconomic context and to race and discusses the effects they have on the ways in which different bodies deal with work, survival, and self-representation. Marc is discussing similar issues, particularly the "tensions between rest, embodiment, race, and temporality that are tied together by an oppressive investment in sleep and supported by an ever-escalating demand for productivity." So perhaps we start with Jamila—if that's OK, Jamila?

JJ-S: Yeah, sure. I'll try not to do a disclaimer. (*Laughs.*) I wrote something in response . . . I'll read it.

(*Pause.*)
Sorry . . .

We're supposed to write a response to this text. I guess I feel as though I'm continually responding to this topic just by breathing. I am thinking about how arguments against productivity—production, function, no product, no function, no productivity—is supposedly being anti-capitalist, and how these things are reductive. I am also thinking about neoliberal capitalism hijacking our innate and constant productivity—so what happens when we refuse ourselves? Every morning I record my dreams, working with sleep as an oracular state, something generative, a tool. I think often about a line someone wrote for a project that I do: "there is no rest; it is a constant act to see without seeing." No off, no relief, no rest. Only more labor. Does this have to be bad? What is resistance when it is not oppositional? A refusal, a denial, or a stop? I would prefer not to. What if choreography is not a corrective[3] but a reframing that happens inside the bodies of those doing and receiving and encountering? No more binaries. I wonder about stripping things back, no frills, no framing, just sleeping in the gallery in 2020. No announcement, no sign, no "About" text. Yes, the risk of arrest, for obstruction, for loitering, for vagrancy, for interrupting the regular flow of things, with your untidy, misplaced punctuation, is no longer a specter. Here it is. We need new grammar. Syntax, another front on which we battle daily. And then, without the embellishments of art framing, has the thing, the reflection space, just been subsumed once again into the quick rhythms and realities of the violent impacts of the system? What does choreography need to become choreography? Does dance need choreography to become art? The other day I read that dolphins can hear in three languages at the same time—we're constantly metabolizing, asleep and awake. I was reminded of someone speaking about my work, advocating for its importance because of its statements and actions around making space for rest, and this being a radical act. They took the example of a work where I was lying on a subwoofer for about 20 or 30 minutes as part of a performance. They saw rest, not doing, in this act of preparation, connecting, channelling. This was annoying and kind of interesting to think about.

KP: Thank you, Jamila.

MA: Thank you so much. I really enjoyed your performative text, Jamila. I want to start by talking about the form of the text, about my experience of reading it, which felt a lot like watching a dance. Each break, each little period felt like it could have been a blackout on stage or perhaps an audible or visible breath taken by a dancer. And I think that kind of breath is very contagious to an audience and that's how your text felt to me. It was this kind of rhythm that was very embodied and created a very specific tempo. So in some ways it was also like you were also writing music. The persistent question, or one of the persistent questions, that I really appreciated in your text was about what comes before performance or what is presumed about a performer or a dancer before the performance even begins. You write "Things that are really about something else, and for other purposes that do not get shared explicitly, or are maybe non-visible, as distinct from what is outwardly proposed"; this was followed by a moment in which you imagined yourself as a kind of Trojan horse, entering the performance space where you have already been interpolated. In another moment you write, "Body that can and will endure the violence of being looked at." Not only were you intentionally creating a space to resist modes of presumptive visibility in the theatre, but you particularly addressed this in relationship to your Blackness as a performer: "the impossibility of living whilst Black" and "the feeling is that I am asked to betray myself, again and again, in order to make space for that self." This complicated sense of your role as a kind of smuggler or Trojan horse feels very real, because you are also alluding to the exhaustion of that process. Quote, "the offence to order, the confusion, the disruption, the anxiety."

I'll end with another sense of resistance that I was moved by, which I think was less about your location but my location as the reader or whoever the reader of this text will be (or perhaps we could even think of them as an audience). I am thinking about how you positioned the reader both as a foreigner, but also as an intimate lover. For example, you write, "As I write this, I am wondering if it makes any sense to you, and I am thinking about the proximities between Blackness and insanity." In another moment you write, "Like your saliva, when we kiss, the smells of you lying next to me in the morning, shaped by proximity that this body will assimilate." As you addressed the reader, and the intimate ways in which your text addressed and invited me in, I was left with the feeling like I was lost in my location. But within this discomfort there was also a sense of possibility. I think I would

AG: end by saying thank you for the vulnerability and the power of that vulnerability that you express in this text.

AG: Thank you, Marc and Jamila. I want to turn to Elena now, and ask you if you would like to do your dialogue with Melissa, or with Usva?

EL: I'll start with Melissa.

AG: Thank you.

KP: Great. This is **Dialogue 5: *Anarchic Inversions of Neoliberal Economies*.**

Melissa offers a performative text about endings and the "end of the world." She bases it on her reading of four performances, which, she suggests, in their "imagining of 'ends' allow dance"— through the manner it "manages to occupy (cultural) space" (Mark Franco)—"to become a prism for politics." She suggests that thinking about the end of the world "offers an opportunity to imagine an elsewhere somewhere after the end" and to question "our current political economic system that makes many of us long for its end."

Elena, reflecting Melissa's longing for the end of the current political economic system, discusses "*how* anarchism offers a different art of living based on mutual aid, or support," which she suggests is one of the things dance communicates. She explains how "Kropotkin's theory of mutual aid explores a way of organizing life that is *neither* based on hierarchies *nor* competition, *nor* restricts movements or celebrates securitisation, all characteristics of our neoliberal times and economies."

EL: First of all, Katerina and Anita, I think you have been all prophetic in setting this a year ago. I was thinking today my goodness, this was set a year ago to happen via Zoom, and here we are, we're all talking via Zoom and it freaked me out! And then I was too busy learning how to use all these platforms over the last week, so I allowed myself this morning to read the essay that I had to respond to, so I opened Melissa's essay.

MBB: Oh god. (*Laughter*)

KP: (*Laughter*)

EL: I think I'll read some of this text because the specific articulation is important. "Sometimes thinking about the end of the world can be exciting. Besides offering some *jouissance* to those of us who enjoy a bit of gallows humor, it offers an opportunity to imagine an elsewhere somewhere after the end. The idea of 'the end' promises a totalizing moment, one that stubbornly stops and forbids the forcefulness of time to barrel on." I thought oh, we're living exactly at this time! We don't even have to imagine it anymore. And then . . . sorry, it was a very beautiful essay to read, also kind of . . . yeah, it left me a little bit breathless, but you have a lot of hope in it, Melissa. For example, when you're talking about the Becky Edmunds' *Goodbye Love* performance, you end with the idea that we continue to live through our parents' past or somebody else's past into the future. I found this hope also in your discussion of the Blaze music video for "Territory," when you were talking about the Algerian men—I think they're refugees?

MBB: Yeah.

EL: . . . and how they dance to the memories of their countries. The other two pieces you write about are also about some form of hope in their imagining of the end of the world—which we're living now. I have a question for you rather than anything much too profound: you have an optimism and a hope and that's very important, but I wonder whether, in the present moment, when we're living something that seems like the end of the world—we don't know yet how it's going to end, or whether anyone's going to live to see the end, you know, who knows—whether this excitement of thinking about the end of the world changes when we are actually in it? When we're living in it. That's the question I had and also the text I was thinking might have been an interesting companion to your own was Lauren Berlant's *Cruel Optimism*.

MBB: (*Nods*)

EL: Having optimism or hope—it is not the same but . . .—carries with it some cruelty. These are the thoughts that first came to mind.

MBB: Thank you. Do I have time to answer to Elena and then respond to her essay?

AG: Yup, we're flowing!

MBB: OK. Yes, that there is a hope ... Well, I always like to think, as Angela Davis says, she's a grand social justice worker, that the point of doing social justice work isn't to see the results necessarily in your lifetime but to plant the seeds so that someone else can see them or to create a post-generational witnessing of the change. So when I was actually writing that about the end, I remember thinking well, for me the end of the world isn't this cataclysmic event that the world literally is going to implode or explode or a comet is coming. It's more like the Anthropocene is going to end, or I see it more as an ideological end to something that must end if we're going to continue in a more compassionate way of being on this planet. So that's why I was thinking about this and in particular aligning my thoughts to the work of, not Afro-pessimism, but Black performance theory and Indigenous world-making—they've been experiencing an end for centuries, right? In my other essay, I talk about Malinche, whose world ended when the Spanish arrived. So then, what do you do, what *can* you do, what *must* you do to put your body into this new configuration? I think that putting our bodies into this new configuration is supposed to be uncomfortable and full of grief, and it's supposed to make us go crazy. I think we have to, we *have* to, because we can't go back—yeah, I don't know. I'm going to get emotional because of everything that's going on ...

In terms of your essay, what I really liked, what I really found useful, particularly reading it now, is mutual aid societies: where am I noticing mutual aid societies right now as this is going on? I've been turning to social media (because I've been so busy I had not been on social media that much, but now, extrovert who needs people company is on social media all the time!). I feel like Instagram has become the mutual aid society for dance, because there are all these dance and DJ parties going on. For example, Ryan Heffington—he's a popular dance choreographer, who has choreographed for Sia and Kenzo and Christine and the Queens—hosts a party, I think in his living room. Mark Kanemura (mkikk808), dancer of *So You Think You Can Dance*, also hosts Instagram parties. He brings out a disco ball, glitter, multi-coloured confetti, and a Gay Pride flag, dresses in rainbow wigs, and creates these parties in his bedroom that you sign on to Instagram Live and dance along. There is also a site called Dancing Alone Together, where every week now they post a schedule of who's hosting a dance class, whether it's ballet barre, Limón technique, or Vogue. Today I saw they had Dominican Bachata. So it's a way of creating community without the physical proximity, but there's that embodied connection that's happening through this . . . It's almost an anarchic revolution of social media, like social media for what it can actually create rather than just sharing of bad news or political views that often don't have any relationship to fact! So I want to thank you for your genealogical sweep through anarchism and mutual aid, because it helped me theorize that which I was experiencing through watching these social media dance videos and performances and observing people's investment in them. I have a colleague in Australia (her Instagram name is @tiny_office_dances) who, using her hands and feet, makes these little dance pieces that fit in the exact square of the Instagram screen. She had made a video using a song I had introduced her to, so she invited me to respond. I decided to be brave because she had tagged me (I'm @mablanc by the way), so I thought "OK, I'm gonna dance back!" I made my own video and now I'm four videos in! We've created this little dance dialogue through this—she theorizes hers, I sort of write autobiographical things. The point I would like to make through this reference to social media performances is that imagination and creativity are ways to think about the ways in which you can *move* through the discomfort of the (*indicates quotes with fingers*) "world ending."

EL: Thank you, Melissa. I don't know much about dance—I think you might have gathered this by reading my essay—but I've been up seeing some performances, so thank you for all the references. One of the things I too was thinking, and also in response to your essay about post-generational witnessing of change or carrying on, is that I see in London an emergence of mutual aid societies that are out helping people in neighborhoods. They have a big one here in Hackney where I live. My colleague, Aviah Day, who started the Hackney Covid-19 Mutual Aid group, messaged us all last Saturday to start a mutual aid society in Hackney and I thought: oh my god, I have never done anything like this in my life! I nevertheless helped set up the Homerton Mutual Aid Group. One of the things I find fascinating and I'm learning how we could do (I mean I'm not an activist so . . .—of course I'll do things in action, but I'm not somebody who organizes things) is how to choreograph. I think we learn how to move, virtually, to people that we don't know and how to connect them and put them together. I think if I hadn't written this piece about dance and mutual aid, I probably wouldn't have been able to actually do it. Somehow, unconsciously, I wrote this specific text. So I will go on Instagram also to look at what dance is doing with this, so thank you very much.

MBB: No problem. I'll send you the links. I'll send you the handles.

EL: Thank you!

MBB: You can dance all day if you want!

(*Laughter*)

AG: Let's hear from Nina (live) and Alexandrina (via video recording) now.

KP: For the recording, we should say that the dialogue we are moving to now is **Dialogue 2: *Commodification of Bodies***. One of the important points Nina makes in her essay is how—and whether—our bodies fit into the capitalist frame and whether they have any power at all. She asks whether we can "reconnect our body to what we feel and express these feelings in a way that also exhibits care."

In some ways Alexandrina echoes these thoughts in her essay. She suggests that in capitalism "powerlessness is capitalized upon and the powerful [are] protected." She foregrounds issues such as the "careless commodification of care and consent" and of overdrafts, censorship, and shame as effects of capitalism on the vulnerable and less privileged individuals and groups.

(*Pause*)

AH: **(video recording)** Hi everyone. I hope everyone's taking care in these . . . times we find ourselves in. Here is my response to Nina's essay, which is entitled "Honesty and the Body." This is my response to it:

> Endless flickering kaleidoscopes of self-portraits posing desperately for "honest" feedback as we try to mentor ourselves out of this inner-outer tornado. Unsatisfied with self—mirror on mirror—do we parade, limping! down the path of mimicry . . . flattering ourselves with AI (yes

misogynist, racially biased but ... emote ... beep ... emotive ... mirror ... mirror ... limp ... limp ...)

The market as parasite. Body as host. Body as inextricable and unextractable from tides of quicksand-capital? Capitalism as a stark, flat line, single point infinity. Get smashed! Get dissolved!

Where can I get a drink and arise from my own insides? Stay close in the fragments. Draw the threads. Shall we stay suspicious, private, and call friends? Keep ourselves as fragments—sink in our fragments before the market owns them as whole. Who stands to gain from these unifications?

That's it—there we have it. Thank you very much and I hope that the dialogue is very, very fruitful. Can't wait to discover where all these things unfold to. So yeah, sending lots of care out to each of you. Thank you very much. Bye.

And thank you to Katerina and Anita for bringing us all together.

NP: Yeah, this was a nice, impressionistic response. I don't know if everyone had the time to read all the essays—in that essay I was thinking through Walter Benjamin's idea of capitalism as religion and his proposition that in capitalism there is an excess of play as opposed to an absence of it. In other words, what if we are actually living in a kind of horrific festival that is never ending, that involves the constant parading of oneself as a performance? So a slightly different idea than the one where we might think of everyday life under capitalism as this kind of dreary, endless thing with these moments of hedonism. What if instead everything is an enforced hedonism of the market, including our every movement? This was the premise of the essay. I want to link this also back to the discussion with Marc—what I was trying to do with the museum and the rave performance pieces was to think about these illicit moments of collective hedonism that were truly, if you like, outside the law. In previous years, I did a lot of work on public order, which Elena (Loizidou) is also very interested in, and it's very interesting to note that something that's happening in Madrid now is the conversion of not only hotels, but also of art spaces into hospitals. So the question that Marc raised about the limits, if you like, of the institution, the parameters of the gallery, let's say, and how rapidly they can be transformed—they are in fact being transformed in this moment. This question also came up a second ago in relation to the question of being together in an embodied way. We currently have enforced social isolation; work and travel have now become a source of great social suspicion. In London, people are posting pictures of people having to travel in the tube packed in together, which has now been infused with a kind of social fear and panic. I'm very interested in this question of the collective and of touch and now we seem further and further away from that possibility. I have been hypothesizing in a slightly crazy way about the idea of a third summer of love.

(*Laughter*)

Obviously the Jeremy Deller film I discuss in my second essay looks at the second summer (if the first summer is '68 or '67/'68 and the second is '89/'90—at least in the UK when we had raves), which is something I remember from my childhood. I grew up in the countryside, in Wiltshire, where rave was happening. I was a little bit too young to be an active hedonistic participant, but it was a very, very, very interesting moment for this elicit or illegal occupation of common land that quickly became even more criminalized, along with repetitive beats, along with the criminalization of nomadism, and was very tied also to the policing of Romany and Traveller people in the UK. The Criminal Justice Bill was proposed in the early Nineties (1994 I think), against all of these things together, and that was in a way, for me, one of the last moments for many people. Deller I think picks up on this in his film. He makes a pedagogical moment of this bringing together of very different people who in a way celebrated their difference through rave, through this collective, euphoric, tactile—in some ways non-sexual, but tactile—experience. I think drugs like MDMA often encourage a certain kind of euphoric tactility, which isn't directly teleologically sexual. I'm quite interested in these forms of, I don't know, even group hugs, those very hippy-ish things . . . but in this current moment, I'm interested also in this social isolation that is being literally imposed and enforced, and people are having to make very personal decisions about who they touch, where they go, how they relate to people on the street. Here (in Madrid) you're allowed out to go to one street; you're allowed out basically once a day to go to the shop and everyone has to stand a meter or a meter-and-a-half away from everybody else. These things change very quickly, so rapidly, and the choreography of the streets, now, walking outside . . . there's a visual pleasure: you look at everybody almost greedily because you know it's the last time you'll see somebody for the day. These random strangers become even more objects of scopophilia and you can see yourself being looked at as well as being, in this way, a source of visual pleasure. I even dressed up a bit today to go to the shop.

(*Laughter*)

So I'm seeking the visual attention of strangers or something! So anyway, this is a rambling series of thoughts!

(*Laughter*)

AG: They're wonderful, thank you!

KP: Yes, thank you! So this last dialogue is **Dialogue 6:** *Escaping Capitalism?*

In her essay, Usva questioned whether we can ever be "free of the logic of consumption," as our everyday performances will "always be based on existing norms." She suggests that what we can do, and what dance can help us do, is "become aware of the power structures guiding and building our reality," because this affords us the opportunity to slowly dismantl[e] the "acculturated normative reiteration of performances."

Elena discusses anarchism, which calls for the "abolition of the state, rules and authority and consequently proposes political economic associations that reflect these ideas." She suggests that Kropotkin's "political economy of mutual aid" is a pathway to such society and discusses mutual aid efforts in the last years (before Covid-19). Considering dance as able to already "teach anarchism about mutual aid," for example, by showing us "how we can come together amongst our differences to create something new," she suggests that dance needs to consider how this kind of mutual aid and support can be repeated throughout all spheres of life. She proposes that anarchism offers pathways to accomplish this.

EL: OK, I can start. Thank you very much for your essay, Usva, I really enjoyed reading it. You bring together the traps of consumption: how they operate on an everyday level and how neoliberalism traps us into consumption. I was just thinking you could have actually had a big part of the conversation with Nina a second ago, because

I think there are similar concerns in your essay. I was also again thinking that what we're trying to do with mutual aid here, in London, are a few things, for example, deliver groceries to people that are vulnerable or in self-isolation. One of the biggest problems, which relates to your question about who gets excluded from this virtual world or virtual platforms or different ways of living, as a result of Covid-19, is that a lot of older people do not have, for example, access to e-banking. Just going back to Nina's comments, the issue becomes what do we do with money, because people are afraid to take money for fear they might be contaminated. There's been a whole discussion about this this morning in mutual aid groups and there is another one as we speak at the Homerton mutual aid group meeting. So I was thinking about these practicalities that make us choreograph in some way, in a different way, our existence; the norms, the ways in which we have learned to operate within neoliberalism and inhabit it ourselves. My only question is, is neoliberalism always so overconsuming? Are there any other spaces that we could find that do things differently, like mutual aid communities? And I'm not saying they do not have issues, but I think it's been interesting for me to see these mutual aid communities, how they are happening now. And actually they're happening very horizontally, to my surprise—I think there are no leaders. People take leads and do things where they have particular skills or they acquire skills while doing them. It's been wonderful to witness (especially while we have a Prime Minister you know, performing sovereignty every day on telly—at this moment on television actually) that we have these kind of horizontal things going on that are doing much more than they (the government) are doing. This is the kind of question I have or a part that I found interesting to converse with your essay.

US: Yeah, thanks, Elena. I think I'll quickly respond to you and then I'll respond to your essay, which I found fascinating. I've been thinking actually very similar things: how this applies to now and especially how it affects vulnerable groups as you said, older people, but also other marginalized groups. We're seeing a lot of mutual aid LGBTQ+ communities also forming because they don't have the same access to, for example, medication and digital consumption. So we are currently seeing a very extreme situation where some people are not allowed to be consumers anymore. This requires a reconfiguration of the ways we can get things we need. We now have to rethink these structures, which ties back to your essay's point, Elena, about having to rechoreograph things. But to answer your question as to whether neoliberalism can not be over-consuming: I've spent most of my academic career looking at consumption and I am pessimistic about it. (*Laughs.*) I think it's never not going to be over-encompassing everything. I've studied a lot of marginalized communities and I've looked at how neoliberal capitalist structures come in; we start off with a community that is not based on neoliberal structures, but then these structures get taken on because of normalization or because of the community's desire to be more recognized in mainstream society. So it is also a matter of whether we want to be recognized by the mainstream society, which is very neoliberal, and how these kind of things fight one another. In my opinion, the way to overcome this is to continuously question it, which brings me back to what I suggest in my essay.

EL: Yeah.

US: We have to continually look at how we can do this differently; how can we fight this? And I think, as you've said, it is coming up a lot in these mutual aid communities that are happening now. They and how people are stepping up and helping are fascinating to me. We live in a culture where we don't know our neighbors, but now, all of a sudden, we're all helping one another.

EL: Yeah, it's quite mysterious how that happens.

US: Yeah.

EL: I've had phone calls from strangers—I've no idea who they were—to ask me how to join the WhatsApp group.

US: Yeah, yeah or—

EL: I don't know how they had my number but they did, so—

US: (*Laughs.*) Yeah, I've found Facebook groups for people in my community and went shopping for people whom I don't know. To respond to your essay—thank you so much, it was a really interesting read. Really fascinating to read about this interaction between anarchism and dance and mutual aid. It got me thinking a lot about these topics of structure versus freedom and how we manage that, and also about what is actually freedom and what is equality; these are things that come up, I think, a lot in your essay. I wonder can we have freedom, freedom from structure, or freedom from choreography, or is this putting new structures in place, new choreographies in place? I was thinking a lot about Judith Butler's work as well when I was reading your essay, because she writes a lot about how agency isn't about escaping normative structures. You can't escape them necessarily, but it is always about building on them in new ways and breaking normatized structures and normative flows of things and doing them in new ways, or not doing them at all. I don't have an answer, but I'm thinking a lot about what freedom is and whether dance can then be fully free in that way. Can dance have no choreography whatsoever, or is it just a new choreography that emerges? And in that sense, do we want to be free from rhythms? Because to engage with other people, we need some sort of rhythms to be able to do things together. But on the other hand, when that rhythm is broken and we have to reconfigure it, I think that's the beautiful part where we have to really become aware of one another and reflect on things together. That is where I think change comes in and what I think we're seeing now while also having to reconfigure how to live our lives in these extreme situations. We're really seeing how people are coming together in new ways. As Melissa was saying earlier in your conversation with her, it is painful, it is uncomfortable, but in some ways I agree that it is necessary, that it's going to hurt, and it's not going to be easy, but that's how change works. So it is about rebuilding these scripts.

I was also thinking a lot about equality, provoked by your essay and in relation to Covid-19. I live in the UK now, but my background is Finnish-Russian. I spent most of my childhood in Finland—we have a lot of welfare there—but also in Russia. A lot of the things we're talking about now with other people from Nordic countries are why things are being done so differently in the UK, how differently equality is perceived in the Nordic countries, and how Nordic countries are set up as welfare states. Our conclusions for the differences between UK and Nordic countries come down to that in welfare states, equality is about complete standardization. This, then, is not in line with how you're talking about equality, a little bit to me perhaps, because

US: in anarchism equality is more about, or that's how I'm reading it, being able to more freely engage and not having standard structures.

EL: Yes.

US: But then a governmental support system actually requires a very strict structure, and I'm just wondering how these would pan out together. I don't know. Maybe it is about figuring out things together again. These are some thoughts I had, but yeah, your essay was really interesting and inspired my thinking, so thank you.

EL: Thank you very much. I don't think I have an immediate answer except that I was thinking about rhythm mainly in terms of how we constantly find ourselves to have to respond to the commands of the neoliberal, capitalist society and that any kind of internal rhythm we have that might be "our own," if we can use that kind of word, kind of gets consumed by that. So I'm not thinking that we should abolish rhythm, but that it is this rhythm that to which we respond, this specific kind of command of doing things. We should be mindful of this in general, whether we're talking about mutual aid societies or whatever. I think there has to be a level of trust, a very old-fashioned way, that when I slow down somebody else might pick up. I don't know how you choreograph that.

US: Yeah, yeah.

EL: I mean some of you are, you know about choreographies more than I do, but I find that interesting, how you find, how you slow down when somebody else speeds up, but then you can come in when somebody else is exhausted, without kind of necessarily having . . .

US: Yeah, it's more like improvising.

EL: . . . an agreement or contract about that. This is what I find interesting when I watch some dance performances: how this is being done. And I don't know how it's being done, but I like . . . yeah, I think sometimes it happens. But it requires, I think, some form of equality or horizontality to bring that also in. Yeah.

And about freedom, I've been thinking all morning about freedom!

US: (*Laughs*)

EL: But I have no answers! What do you do with this idea of freedom when you are trapped in your house? How do you expand, how can you demand for it when the demand is to be unfree at this point?

US: And also the good thing for others now, for the good of everyone, is *not* to be free.

EL: Yeah, but also, going back to Melissa's essay, without losing this idea of: I'm not moving for the sake of others as opposed to restricting others from moving (as it happens in Greece with the refugee migrants who are trying to move across borders, but have been held there). So how do you think about all these things without making generalizations, I guess? That's what I've been thinking about this morning, without any conclusions, but that's what has been on my mind.

KP: Thank you very much, Elena and Usva.

AG: That's wonderful, yeah.

KP: So the "equation" of bodies, movement, and political economies, what this book seems to be about, has been reshaped by Covid-19 and to some extent I think Covid-19 has accentuated the importance of each of these elements and their interrelation.

AG: The book now seems to be political economies: dance and the end of the world.

(*Laughs*)

How people respond to it, right?

KP: Yes, perhaps! Does anybody have any thoughts on what has been discussed so far?

AG: What about process, because we didn't frame it at all in terms of why we're having this conversation!

(*Laughs*)

We're having this conversation because the series is called *Dance in Dialogue*, and at the time when we imagined it, we thought oh, we'll have online conversations instead of in person to ensure we can be together in time if being together also in space is difficult. Now it's this imperative place where everybody is having these online conversations, but the idea was to exchange ideas. I'm interested in where you would place the ideas, now that you've heard everybody speak.

(*Pause*)

Would you revise your essay, would you like to think about what it would be like to just excerpt what we've talked about? How has this conversation enhanced your perspective on the work that you've already done? I guess that's the way to put it?

US: I think it would be really fascinating to just document this to be honest. I don't know if I would want to go back and revise things. I think it's fascinating to hear how people responded to my work and then if someone was to read this conversation, they would need to read my original essay to see what people responded to. I'd be quite interested in seeing how we can document this conversation for the purpose of the book.

MA: Yeah, equally, as a historian and scholar, I think it is always really tricky to . . . it's not to say that we would go back and directly address what's going on right now, it's hard not to, but it is . . .

(*Connection cuts out*)

AG: OK, perhaps someone else can respond until he comes back on. I'll text him.

MBB: I liked this exchange between Usva and Elena, particularly the conversation about rhythm. I kept thinking about the uses of improvisation and how improvisation, as a tool for dance-making or for choreography, is so important, because it teaches you the skill of adapting your own sense of your embodied rhythm—whether it's ingrained through training or ingrained through your cultural background—and how you have to attune or not to the other body dancing with you. You are constantly making these negotiations of when and when not to attune and come together. I think that we're seeing this now on a macro scale in terms of everybody has their daily rhythms, their life rhythms, and the ways that our bodies would like to be moving, but we're being managed (*laughs*) by this pandemic and by the multiple locations where the state government or the federal government or the city government is telling you what you can and cannot do. But even in this case, there are still ways in which you are maintaining a sense of rhythm. So I think it's kind of a new training regimen that we're getting used to. I'm just trying to think through dance: it's a new training regimen we're getting used to, and, again, it hurts, it's uncomfortable. If you think about: oh, I'm going to start lifting weights, the day after you lift weights your body needs to be in ice, right? So I think it's this attunement. Sara Ahmed writes a lot about attunement and coming into, to attune to other people. I think this is what is slowly starting to emerge, this way of—we have to take care of the other; not the other as something different than me, or something outside of me, but the other as connected to me in terms of the everyday vicissitudes of existence . . . I don't know if that makes any sense!

US: Yeah, it does, yeah.

KP: I also keep thinking about listening, because attuning is also to me listening with, well, your ears, but generally with your body and senses.

MBB: Your body, yeah.

KP: Listening keeps coming to me as an idea and I also keep thinking that we need to listen intently to what's going on because this could lead to something really fantastic (for example the realization that capitalism needs to end, that we must take care of one another in many ways, and that slower rhythms, universal health care, and universal basic income are necessary). But I'm also thinking about the terrifying ways (we saw Italy recently using the army to keep people locked down, for example) in which this can all go very wrong. What if somebody shuts down social media and we can't . . . or the internet. . . . So listening, being able to listen to one another, attuning to one another in different ways, I think is really crucial. Yeah. Sorry for the horrifying scenarios I presented . . . (*Laughter*)

MBB: Yeah, and then the question of whether, at least whether I would rewrite—I think I'd like to leave it as is because it is a historical document. It was written at a particular time and then now the discussion is helping to see the ways in which it could develop or the urgency should it need to develop, or just leave as is because it needs to exist as that document from November 2019. I don't know.

AG: Thank you. That's really helpful.

MBB: I mean there's time to rewrite. I'm not saying that I don't have the time necessarily to rewrite.

(*Laughter*)

KP: For me it *is* about tracking how this, what the impact is of what is happening. I think there's value in that, yeah.

US: Yeah.

AG: So we can frame it also, obviously we'll have to frame the volume, maybe Katerina can talk about next steps?

KP: Yes. The next step is for us to get back to you with final comments on your essays. Then this document is being recorded and we'll transcribe it, and then, I think, Anita and I will initially discuss how we want to include it, whether it's just going to be exactly this, what we're hearing now, with some edits, or whether we want to develop it in some way. I'm not quite sure yet. You're welcome to send us ideas if you think of something that can work well.

And then we need to write the Introduction and start finalizing things. The aim is to submit the manuscript in July 2020. We don't want to rush completing it because I think this conversation is important; so I think we're going to spend some time figuring it out.

AG: Also, we want to have a launch and we don't know if people can travel in September 2020.

US: Or even go to a bookstore, right?

AG: Right!

(*Laughter*)

KP: I don't know how I'm going to handle it if we are still in lockdown in September . . .

US: I agree!

MBB: I need to get to Greece, Katerina, I need to get to Greece!

KP: Ah Melissa, I was thinking about texting you about this!

MBB: OK, text me separately, yeah, we'll talk.

KP: So hopefully . . . I don't know. I also don't want to rush into being free because I think there's value in this lack of . . . in this new configuration; there are some things that are coming out that are very important for us to realize. I don't know, including—

MBB: I agree, I agree. Well, because when you think about it, when you, for example, give your students or yourself a choreographic task, "make a 90-second piece where you have to walk in a straight line but you can't repeat your steps," within those limits there's a lot of potential; but the potential emerges *from* this limitation. So I don't know . . . that's how I'm trying to see this!

AG: Welcome back, Marc!

MA: Hi, I'm so sorry. I got kicked off the internet. Sorry about that.

KP: Welcome back, Marc. We were saying that we're hoping for a September 2020 launch for this book and for the book series. For this, the idea is that as many of you as possible participate in person or, if in person is not possible, via Zoom. We'll invite you to the launch and also perhaps invite you to contribute, if you want, with a short talk about your experience of participating in this book project or to share some of your writing.

And thank you for staying an extra half-hour—we know that's a lot of time!

EL: Oh wow! It felt like nothing actually!

US: It was really interesting, yeah.

AG: It was really nice to hear everybody—we got a lot of new ideas out—and also just to hear people's responses was fantastic. Thank you, all.

MBB: Thank you for sharing that document, because it makes me excited about reading everybody else's essays that I haven't had a chance to look at—but I will now!

KP: Thank you very much, everyone. Alright. We can do this (referring to Covid-19).

MBB: Yeah, stay safe everyone.

MA: Stay safe.

MBB: Wash your hands!

(*Laughter*)

Var: Bye bye.

(*End of recording.*)

Notes

1 The texts referenced in this conversation are the chapters in this volume by Marc Arthur, Melissa Blanco Borelli, Alexandrina Hemsley, Elena Loizidou, Nina Power, Usva Seregina, and Jamila Johnson-Small. The videos mentioned are from the video playlist in Katerina Paramana and Anita Gonzalez, "Opening Thoughts and Introductions" (this volume).

2 Judith Butler, *Notes Towards a Performative Theory Assembly* (Cambridge: Harvard University Press, 2015), 96–7.

3 Marc is discussing choreography as a "corrective" in the essay to which Jamila is responding here.

CONTRIBUTORS

Editors and Contributors

Katerina Paramana (Brunel University London, UK): sociopolitical and ethical dimensions of performance; political economy, affect and collectivity; biopolitics and neoliberal capitalism; continental philosophy.

Anita Gonzalez (University of Michigan, USA): performance and cultural studies; African diaspora studies; dance studies; maritime performance.

Foreword Contributor

Tavia Nyong'o (Yale University, USA): ethics and aesthetics of social and cultural analysis; visual, musical, and performative dimensions of Blackness; dimensions of modern regimes of race.

Essay and Group Conversation Contributors

From Performance Studies and Dance:

Marc Arthur (University of Michigan, USA): performance and diversity, equity and inclusion, dramaturgies of transformation; new forms of biomedical embodiment.

Melissa Blanco Borelli (University of Maryland, College Park, USA): dance and politics, feminist historiography, Black performance theory, Latin American popular dance.

Alexandrina Hemsley and Jamila Johnson-Small (Project O, UK): UK collaborating artists exploring the political in dance and performance practice.

From Political Theory/Economics/Social Theory:

Elena Loizidou (Birkbeck, University of London, UK): political theory; law and culture; gender and sexuality; politics and ethics of Judith Butler's work.

Nina Power (Independent Scholar, UK): social theory; cultural criticism; European philosophy; feminism and politics.

Usva Seregina (Goldsmiths, University of London, UK): economics; consumer culture; experiences of art; aesthetics; fantasy.

ABOUT THE EDITORS

Katerina Paramana is Senior Lecturer (Associate Professor) in Theatre and Performance at Brunel University London. Her interdisciplinary research is concerned with the sociopolitical and ethical dimensions of contemporary performance and of experimental theater and dance. It brings into conversation performance, critical theory, political economy, continental philosophy, and cultural and social theory. She is co-editor of *Art and Dance in Dialogue* (2020) and her articles have been published in journals including *Performance Research*, *Contemporary Theatre Review*, *Dance Research*, and GPS: *Global Performance Studies*. Recent publications include "The Animation of Contemporary Subjectivity" (*Performance Research*) and "The Contemporary Dance Economy" (*Dance Research*). Her performances have been presented in theaters and gallery spaces in the United States, United Kingdom, and Europe.

Dr. Paramana was awarded the BRIEF Research Award (BRUNEL RESEARCH INITIATIVE AND ENTERPRISE FUND) 2019–20. She was an Associate Researcher with *Performance Matters* (2009–13), a four-year AHRC funded creative research project investigating the cultural value of performance, directed by Adrian Heathfield, Gavin Butt, and Lois Keidan, and a Participating Artist of Sadler's Wells Summer University (2015–18), which was led by Jonathan Burrows and Eva Martinez. Paramana is co-founder and series co-editor of the interdisciplinary book series *Dance in Dialogue* (Bloomsbury Academic), on the *techne* Peer Review College (AHRC Doctoral Training Partnership), and on the Editorial Board of the *Body, Space, & Technology* journal. She has served on the Executive Committee of the Society for Dance Research and on the Board of Directors of Performance Studies International (PSi) (2016–19) (katerinaparamana.com).

Anita Gonzalez (PhD, University of Wisconsin) is Associate Dean for Faculty Affairs and Professor of Theatre and Drama. Her recent academic publications are in the fields of African diaspora studies, dance studies, and maritime performance. Anita has authored two books, *Afro-Mexico: Dancing between Myth and Reality* (2010) and *Jarocho's Soul* (2005) and co-edited the volume *Black Performance Theory* (2013). Her essays about multicultural and international performance appear in several edited collections including *Narratives in Black British Dance* (Akinyele), *Black Acting Methods* (Luckett), *Community Performance Reader* (Kuppers), *Festive Devils* (Riggio, Segura, and Vignola) and the *Oxford Handbook of Dance and Theatre* (George-Graves, 2015). She has published articles in the *Radical History Review*, *Modern Drama*, *Performance Research International*, *Theatre Symposium*, and *Dance Research Journal*.

Gonzalez has completed three Senior Scholar Fulbright grants and been awarded a residency at Rockefeller's Bellagio Center in Italy. She was a Humanities Center Fellow at the University of Michigan during the 2017/18 academic year and she is a recent recipient of the Shirley Verrett Award for outstanding teaching of performance. Gonzalez is a member of the National Theatre Conference, Lincoln Center Director's Lab, League of Professional Women in Theatre, and the Regional Representative for The Dramatists Guild. Dr. Gonzalez is currently a member of the Executive Committee of the University of Michigan Press and a co-series editor for the interdisciplinary book series *Dance in Dialogue* at Bloomsbury Academic.

INDEX

125th and Freedom: Public Performance Ritual (Golden, 2017)   9, 143, 146–7, 148 n.12

Abozao del Pacífico   92
Abramović, Marina   72, 156
Acid Corbynism   8
Acosta, Navild   71, 74–7
ACT UP   9, 47–9, 154
Adewole, Funmi   33
aesthetic performance   32–5, 138
affect transmission   50, 51
African diasporic dance   35
afterlives   92–5, 98
Agamben, Giorgio   93, 119, 122, 128 n.3
Agape (FlucT, 2012)   77
Ahmed, Sara   177
AIDS   46–51, 154, 155
Alí, Maurizio   100 n.11
Alliez, Éric   23
Ambien   73, 74, 76
anarchism and dance   119–24, 143–5, 147, 163, 166, 170, 172, 173
"Anarchism: What It Really Stands For" (Goldman)   122
anarcho-communism   124–6
antiauthoritarianism   119
Antioquia, Colombia   93
Arbery, Ahmaud   2
Arcadia (Wright, 2018)   8
Arthur, Marc   153–7, 160–3, 168, 176, 179

art(s)   23, 24, 86
  collection   77, 156
  impact of political economies   33
  of living   119, 121, 163
  performance   6, 72, 156
  practice   5, 66
  in society   127
Arts and Humanities Research Council   99
Atlantic Reconciliation Station   75
attunement   176, 177
audience participation   103, 106
Auslander, Philip   106

Balboa, Vasco Núñez de   92
ballet   35
Barondess, Joseph   120, 121
Battery Dance Company   49
Bauer, Gary   50
Bed Piece (Burden, 1972)   72
Bengolea, Cecilia   77
Benjamin, Walter   57, 58, 168
Berardi, Franco "Bifo"   12 n.12, 25, 98
Bergson, Henri   113
Berlant, Lauren   154, 164
Bharatanatyam dancer   33
Bidet, Jacques   23–4
Black and Global Majority people   2
Black Lives Matter protests   4
Blackness   82, 162
Black Power Naps (Acosta and Sosa, 2018)   71, 74–7

Black
    artists   33, 66
    free   92
    women   125
The Blaze   8, 112–14, 164
bodies   41, 48, 51, 55, 56, 63
    Black   75
    collective   35, 42, 43, 45
    honest   59, 60
    and political economies   6, 17–20, 37
    sleeping   71, 76
    in space   103–5, 139, 153, 156–7
bodily connection   138–40, 142 n.28
"body of the state"   44
Borden, Iain   140
Borelli, Melissa Blanco   21, 153, 157–60, 163–7, 173, 175–80
Bourdieu, Pierre   23, 33
Boyle, Michael Shane   23
Brexit referendum   19
British National Boat Institute   126
Brooks, Rayshard   2
Burden, Chris   72
Burt, Ramsay   22
Butler, Judith   156, 173

capital and markets   21
capitalism   3, 4, 23, 57, 58, 63, 64, 125–7, 145–7, 167, 168, 177
    contemporary   20, 73, 101
    Foucault's critique of   21, 24
    neoliberal   3, 18, 19, 21, 24, 41, 111, 153, 161, 172, 174
    racial   76
capitalist economies   2, 6, 63, 64, 96, 153
capitalist patriarchy   65, 66
care   59, 64, 68, 95, 167
Casa de Cultura, Unguía   92, 95, 96
Castro, Mónica   94
Cavarero, Adriana   156

Cave, Nick   75
Chaignaud, François   77
chance movement   145
Chocó/Urabá region, Colombia   93–4
choreography   19, 20, 48, 63, 68 n.4, 76, 77, 95–6, 116, 144–6, 161, 173, 174, 176
    folkloric   97
    pharmacological   74
choreopoetics   147
cimarrones   92
Citará   92
class   19–21, 23, 35–7, 106
    behavior   34
    categories   35
    hierarchies   34
    origins   32
    structures   135
    struggle   21, 24
collective dance   59
Colombian armed conflict   93–4, 98, 158–9
Colombian Institute of Anthropology and History (ICANH)   94, 98
Colombian peace accords (2016)   93–4
colonialism   92–4, 116
communication   6, 63, 122, 124
concert performances   33, 36
consumer
    roles   133–5, 140
    society   133, 135, 136, 138, 139, 140
consumption   133, 134, 140, 170, 172
    as freedom and constraint   134–7
contemporary culture   139
contemporary dance   20, 35, 36, 77
contemporary political economy   6, 20, 24, 25, 37
contemporary society   127, 135, 136, 140
contextualization   106

control 42, 51
convivencia 92–8, 157
Cotton bullet collective 9
Covid-19 1, 2, 4, 6, 152, 153, 155, 171, 173, 175
Cramer, Peter 48, 49
Crary, Jonathan 73
Criminal Justice Bill (1994) 169
cultural capital 23, 33, 106, 136
Cunningham, Merce 8, 143, 145, 147
Cvejić, Bojana 9, 41, 42, 44, 45, 101, 106
cynicism 59

dance academia 27 n.14
dance and movement 44, 45, 74, 76, 77, 95, 97, 107, 119, 122, 123, 158
dance festival 92–4, 96, 98
dance practices 5, 33
dance professionals and political economies 32–3
dancer's life 123
dance studios 32, 33, 35
dance technique 49, 74
"Dancing Darkey Boy" 36
danza actual o el evento coreográfico: estructuras temporales para provocar un evento imposible (nibia pastrana santiago, 2015) 112, 114–16
Dariena, Colombia 92, 96, 157
Darwin, Charles 124
Davis, Angela 3, 165
Dawson, Richard 59
Day, Aviah 166
Deller, Jeremy 9, 43–5, 156, 169
De Smedt, Christine 9, 41, 42, 44, 45, 101, 106
Desmond, Jane 21
DiMaggio, Paul 34
displacement 92, 93, 98, 157, 158

Dominguez Mejía, Marta 99
dreaming 75–7
duality 102–3

economic access 33–6
economic equality/inequality 3, 36, 122, 123, 147
economic management 72–4
economic policies 50, 71
Edmunds, Becky 9, 112–13, 164
Embera Cuti community 92, 94, 96, 97
embodiment 6, 22, 41, 63, 101, 102, 162
emotions 51, 63
End of Eating Everything, The (Mutu + Santigold, 2013) 8, 112, 117–18
equal access 48, 135, 139
equality/inequality 33, 173–4. *See also* economic equality/inequality
ethics 17–19, 33
ethnicity 36
eudaimonia 17, 18
Euro-American dance 33
Everybody in the Place (Deller, 2018) 9, 43, 44, 156
everyday life performance 136–8
evolution, theory of 124
Exchange (Cunningham, 1978) 8, 143–7
experimental drugs 47
Eyaquera 94

Falsnaes, Christian 8, 103
fascism 24
Federal Drug Administration (FDA) 47, 48, 50
financial crises (2009) 19
Floyd, George 2
FlucT 77

FORCE (Falsnaes, 2018)   8, 101, 103–5
Foster, Susan Leigh   48
Foucault, Michel   71–3, 76
Franko, Mark   50, 51, 111
freedom   44, 58, 121–3, 135, 139, 143, 146, 147, 156, 173
free-market economy   71, 72, 96, 133, 136
"Fulfilment Centre" (Dawson, 2019)   59
funding   5, 95, 96, 98, 160

Galas, Diamanda   154
Galindo, Regina José   8, 49–51, 154
gender   34–7
gestures   33, 35, 55, 59, 95, 101, 113–14, 119, 145
Golden, Ebony Noelle   9, 143, 146, 147
Goldman, Emma   119–23
Gómez-Barris, Macarena   95
Gonzalez, Anita   17, 18, 76, 92, 123, 125, 127, 135, 139, 143, 147, 152, 153, 156, 157, 163, 164, 168, 175–6, 178
Gonzalez, Jonathan   8
Goodbye, Love (Edmunds, 2015)   9, 112–13, 164
Great Migration   146, 148 n.12
group conversation   151–80
group existence   43
Gržinić, Marina   22
Guasapura, María   96
Guatemala   50
guilt   58–9
Guna Tule, Arquía   92, 95–6, 99 n.4

Hackney Covid-19 Mutual Aid group   166
Haraway, Donna   98, 116
Harney, Stefano   20
Harrell, Trajal   71, 73, 76
Hartman, Sadiya   125

Harvey, David   12 n.13, 23
Haus der Kulturen der Welt, Berlin   73
health services   134
Heffington, Ryan   165
Hemsley, Alexandrina   167
Hölscher, Stefan   22
Homar, Susan   116
homeland   113
Homerton Mutual Aid Group   166, 171
Hsieh, Techching   72

identity   134, 135, 139
   politics   19, 31 n.61
ideology   50–1
illusion   138, 140
Imhof, Anne   77
indigenous communities   93–5
individualism   34
insomnia   73, 75
Instagram   165–7

Johnson-Small, Jamila   157, 160–1

Kanemura, Mark   165
Kelleher, Joe   23
Kershner, Jacob   120
Kisselgoff, Anna   144
knowledge and dance   139
Kolb, Alexandra   22
Kropotkin, Peter   120, 124–7, 143, 147 n.2, 163, 170
Kunst, Bojana   22
Kusserow, Adrie   34

labor   25, 34, 84, 97, 126, 136
La Malinche   98, 165
Lazzarato, Maurizio   23
leadership   66
Lepecki, André   73, 74
Lesvos   126
LGBTQ+ community   142 n.28, 171
limitations of dance   147

Live Art Development Agency   66
Loizidou, Elena   163, 164, 166–8, 170–2, 174–6, 179
Loveless, Natalie   112

McDade, Tony   2
Marshall, Alfred   18, 122
Marshall, Peter   125
Martin, Randy   22
Marx, Karl   57
Marxist class-theory   20, 24
Mbembe, Achille   93
Médecins Sans Frontières (MSF)   126
Mendieta, Ana   49
Mendoza, Omar   95–6
Merce Cunningham Dance Company   144
Metsä (Cotton bullet collective)   9
Midgelow, Vida   21
Ministry of Culture, Colombia   94, 95, 98, 99 n.9
"Mo Chara"   126
modernity   57, 58
Most, John   120
Moten, Fred   20
Museum of Modern Art (MoMA, New York City)   72, 156
Museum of Modern Art Kiasma, Helsinki   103
Mutu, Wangechi   8, 112, 117–18
mutual aid   119, 120, 124–7, 143–5, 147, 163, 170
    groups   142 n.28, 171, 172
    societies   165, 166
Mutual Aid (Kropotkin)   124, 147 n.2

necropower   93
neoliberalism   4, 24, 72–4, 94–5, 122, 123, 125, 127, 133, 170–2
Nobel Peace Prize   126–7
noetic processes   24, 25
nomadism   169
non-naturalized performance   102

Nordic countries   173
norms   102–4, 136–8
North Americans   34
"Notes on Gesture" (Agamben)   119
nudity   104
Nyong'o, Tavia   75

One Year Performance (Hsieh, 1978–9)   72

Paggett, Taisha   8
palenques   92
Panamá City   92
Paramana, Katerina   5, 6, 36, 59, 76, 91, 122, 127, 135, 143, 147, 152, 154, 156, 159–61, 163, 168, 175, 177–9
parkour   34
pastrana santiago, nibia   8, 112, 114–16
People of Color   74–6
performance knowledge   139, 140
Performance Space, New York   74
philia   25
Pinkins, Tonya   5
political violence   49, 93, 95, 98
polytemporality   75, 76
Power, Nina   153–7, 167–71
powerlessness   64, 167
power structures   3, 101, 102, 104–6, 133, 134, 136–8, 140, 157
Precarious Workers Brigade (BWB)   127
Prickett, Stacey   22
private property   45, 124–6
productivity   83, 161
Project O   64–7, 81
proletarianized consumer   21, 24

race   34–7, 75, 160
racism   1–3, 25
Rackete, Carola   126

INDEX   **189**

rage   46–51, 154–5
rave   43, 44, 45, 169
Read, Alan   23
reality   33, 63, 101, 103, 107, 136–40
Refugee Rescue   126
refugee rescue operations   126
Regan, Ronald   49, 50
resistance   46, 48–50, 63, 162
rest   83, 161
Restrepo Jaramillo, Isabel   99
rhythms   20, 33, 145–7, 158, 162, 173, 174, 176, 177
Ridout, Nicholas   23
Ríos Montt, Efraín   49, 50
Romany and Traveller people   169
Roy, Arundhati   3
Ruiz, Sandra   116

Santa María la Antigua del Darién. *See* Darienta, Colombia
Santigold   8, 112, 117–18
Schechner, Richard   137–9
Schneider, Rebecca   113
Scott, Anna   36
Sea-Watch   126
second summer of love (1988–9)   43
Second World War   72
Sehgal, Tino   156
"Seize the FDA" (1988)   9, 47–9
self-commodification   136, 138–9
self-conceptualization   72
self-reflection   102
sensations   63, 68 n.4, 139
Seregina, Usva   157–60, 163, 170–9
sexual violence   64
Shoot (Burden, 1971)   72
Siegmund, Gerald   22
site specific performances   77
skin color   35
sleep   71–7, 161
Sloterdijk, Peter   154
social behaviors   72

social forces   50–1
social media performances   165, 166, 177
social movements   24
socioeconomic status   20, 106
Sosa, Fannie   71, 74–7
Southeast Asian dance   35
sovereignty   93
So You Think You Can Dance (TV show)   165
Spatial Confessions (Cvejić and de Smedt, 2014)   9, 41–4, 101–2, 104, 105, 156, 159
Stiegler, Bernard   21, 24, 25
Stojnić, Aneta   22
street dancer   33
street performance   146
subject positions   33
survival   47–9, 118, 124, 125, 127

Tamayo Duque, Anamaría   99
Tate Live's Performance Room   41
Taylor, Breonna   2
"Territory" (The Blaze, 2017)   8, 112–14, 164
theater and politics   23
Tickle the Sleeping Giant (Harrell, 2001–12)   71, 73, 76
Tierra (Galindo, 2013)   8, 49–50, 154
tourist economy   94, 99 n.9
"Tracking the Political Economy of Dance" (Desmond)   21
trauma   64, 65
Trump, Donald   19
Truth Commission   94
Tudor, David   144
Turner, Victor   138

Underground Railroad   146, 148 n.12
Unguía, Colombia   93–5, 99 n.4
United Kingdom   2, 3, 19, 20, 35, 43, 169, 173

United States   2, 5, 19, 32–5, 49, 74, 120, 125
"university services"   136
use-value   84
Uytterhoeven, Lise   21

Van Assche, Annelies   22
Vaugham, David   144
Vélez, Mauricio   95
voluntary associations   125

wage system   125–7
war crimes   49
Waters, Jack   48, 49
Weber, Max   58

Weeks, Kathi   18, 25
We See You (campaign)   5
West, Cornel   3
Western culture   159
white supremacy   65, 66
William, Tennessee   87 n.1
Wilson, August   5
women and dance   122–3
working class   120, 121
Wright, Paul   8

Young Boy Dancing Group   77

Žižek, Slavoj   12 n.13, 24

www.ingramcontent.com/pod-product-compliance
Lightning Source LLC
Chambersburg PA
CBHW070637300426
44111CB00013B/2145